enquiry geography

BOOK 1

Christine **W** *inter*

Brian **G** *reasley*

Eleanor **W** *illiamson*

Graham **R** *anger*

Hodder & Stoughton

LONDON SYDNEY AUCKLAND TORONTO

Acknowledgements

The authors and publishers thank the following for permission to reproduce photographs and material in this book (the numbers refer to the pages on which the material appears.):
Keith Grimwade 6, 9, 13. Dr. R Evans 8. Barnabys Picture Library 11 B & C, 29, 78. Holt Studios/Nigel Cattlin 11D, 12. Britain on View 16 top left, 28. Paul Taverner 16 top and bottom right. Alan Howard 16 middle. Spectrum 16 bottom left, 71, 92 bottom. Hepworth Building Products 20. Valley News Pictures 24. The Guardian 25. Popperfoto 26. Topham 30, 83. Reed Midland Newspapers Ltd, Worcester 33. J Allan Cash 45, 48, 80, 92 middle. GW Moss 46, 51. The Great Central Rail Tour, Silver Star Books 1988 54. Winter & Kidson 57. The Houses Game by Jeff Bishop and Graham Russell, Resources for Learning Development Unit, Bristol 59. Chorley and Handford 62. Picturepoint 63. Trevor White 64. Barnsley Metropolitan Borough Council 66–69. Koyo Holdings 67. Janet and Colin Bird/Wales Scene 70. Yorkshire Water 71. Deutsche Presse Agentur 76. Greenpeace 79. US Geological Survey 86 top. FAO 86. Cephas 92 top. David Davies/Bruce Coleman Ltd 93 top. John Topham/Bruce Coleman Ltd 93 middle. French Tourist Board 93 bottom. John Chaffey 94. The remaining photographs were supplied by the authors. The Ordnance Survey maps on pages 4, 19, 47, 53 and 64 have been reproduced with the permission of the controller of HMSO, Crown Copyright Reserved.

Every effort has been made to contact the holders of copyright material but if any have been inadvertently overlooked the publisher will be pleased to make the necessary alterations at the first opportunity.

British Library Cataloguing in Publication Data
Enquiry geography.
   Bk. 1
   1. Great Britain. Geography
   I. Greasley, Brian
   910.71241
   ISBN 0–340–54634–4

First published 1991

Typeset by Taurus Graphics, Abingdon, Oxon.
Illustrated by Hardlines, Charlbury, Oxford.
Printed in Hong Kong for the educational publishing division of Hodder and Stoughton Ltd, Mill Road, Dunton Green, Sevenoaks, Kent by Colorcraft Ltd.

Contents

WHERE WE LIVE

"Hi! I'm Anna and this is Daniel. We both live in Reach, a small village near Cambridge in East Anglia."

"We both wanted to find out more about the local area and region in which we live. We started by looking at an Ordnance Survey map of the local area. From this we made a list of questions we hoped to answer."

Location of Reach

North Sea

Glasgow • Edinburgh

Newcastle-upon-Tyne

Belfast

Leeds

Liverpool • Manchester

Dublin

Birmingham   Reach

Cardiff • Bristol

Southampton   London

0 — 150 km
0 — 100 miles

Ordnance Survey map showing Reach © Crown copyright

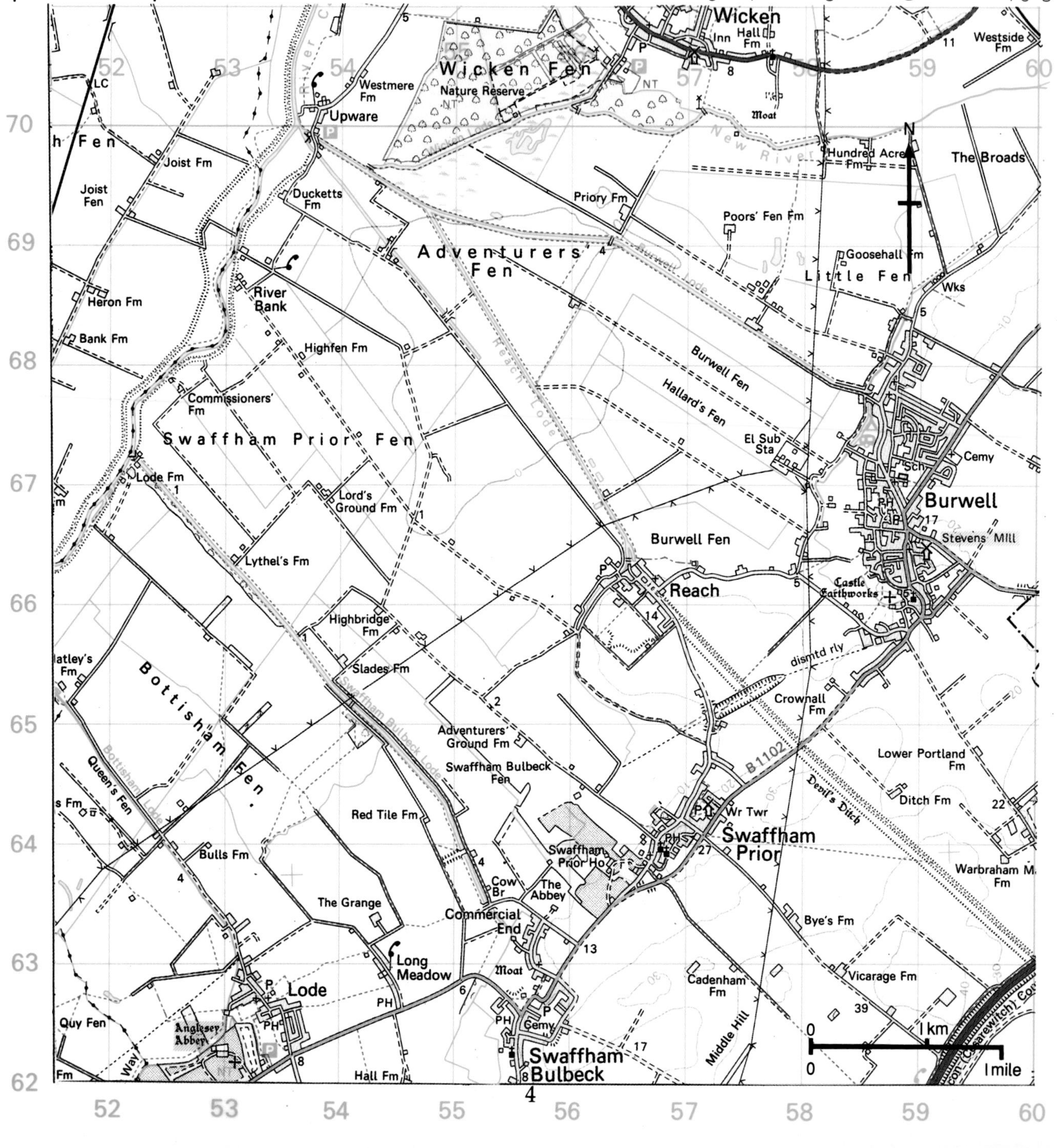

4

Here is our list of questions.

1. Did the local area always look like it does today?
2. Why is the land to the west of the village so different from the land to the east of the village?
3. Why was the village built at this location?
4. What do we mean by the region of East Anglia?
5. Has all of East Anglia the same landscape?
6. What changes are taking place in the work of the people of East Anglia?
7. What changes are taking place in the towns and villages of East Anglia?
8. What changes are taking place in transport in East Anglia?
9. Is there a place which can be called the centre of the region?

Part of Wicken Fen, now a National Trust property, which shows how the Fens looked in the past. The windmill was used as a drainage pump.

1. Did the local area always look like it does today?

"I can remember Adventurers' Fen before it was drained. It was a wilderness of water and reeds. Old John Harrison lived there. He caught fish and eels with a three-pronged spear, or in bottle-shaped baskets.

Wildfowl, ducks and geese lived on the fen in great flocks. John would shoot them using a punt with a large gun fixed to it. He could glide without a ripple through the water to get near to the birds.

The reeds were cut for thatching the houses in the village. The peat would be cut and dried out to use for burning on the fire in the houses.

I remember fen donkeys and horses pulling the barges full with goods for the village along the **lodes**. These were the old canals linking the villages to the rivers."

The memories of an old man in Reach.

1 Find the village of Reach on the Ordnance Survey map. Copy and complete the following:
(a) _____ is in grid square 5666.
(b) Upware is in grid square _3_0.
(c) Upware is north _____ of Reach.
(d) Reach Post Office is _____ kilometres in a straight line from the disused windmill ⚑ in Burwell.
(e) Reach is _____ metres above sea level.
(f) The land in grid square 5466 is metres above sea level.
2 Describe the route you would take along the roads from Reach to Upware (use directions to help you).
3 Write two sentences to describe what the Fens were like 200 years ago.
4 Join with a friend to make a list of questions you would like to ask about your home area.

Different Lands

" We have been trying to work out the answers to two questions. Why is the land to the west of the village so different from the land to the east of the village? "

" And why was the village built at this location? "

Chalk landscape

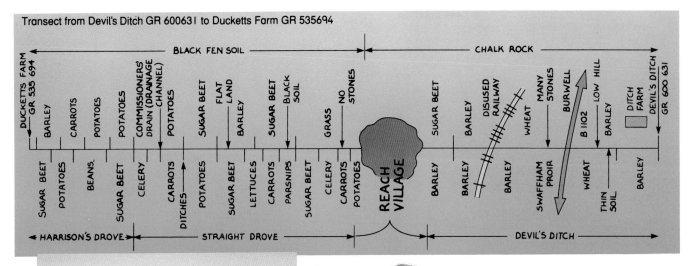

Transect from Devil's Ditch GR 600631 to Ducketts Farm GR 535694

BLACK FEN SOIL — CHALK ROCK

HARRISON'S DROVE — STRAIGHT DROVE — DEVIL'S DITCH

Fen landscape

We began by walking from the south west of Devil's Ditch to Ducketts Farm. We noted on a map what we saw on the way. This is called a transect. We did this to find all the main features to the west and the east of the village.

We drew a cross section of our transect using the heights shown on the map.

Reach grew up on the Fen edge. Goods could be brought to the village along the lode. The village was on higher dry chalk land. People could cut reeds for thatch and catch wildfowl for food from the Fen. They could grow crops and graze animals on the chalk land. The chalk could be used for building. There was a spring at the edge of the chalk.

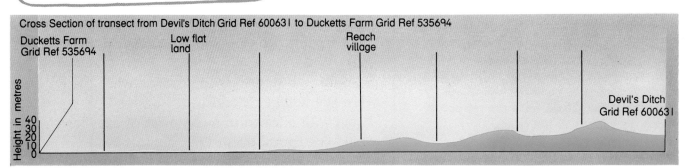

Cross Section of transect from Devil's Ditch Grid Ref 600631 to Ducketts Farm Grid Ref 535694

Ducketts Farm Grid Ref 535694

Low flat land

Reach village

Devil's Ditch Grid Ref 600631

Height in metres
40
30
20
10
0

We found that the land from Reach Village to Ducketts Farm was very flat.

Well you would, that's Adventurers' Fen. It used to be all marshland and reed beds. The fen was drained about 200 years ago. You can see what it was like at Wicken Fen, the only bit of old fen left.

There were a lot of ditches there.

Oh yes, well there would be if it were drained marsh. You can see the drainage channels on the map. Very low too, some only 1 metre above sea level.

We saw a lot of different crops growing.

The rotted vegetation makes fertile soil which is well drained and easily worked. All kinds of vegetable and grain crops grow there. The fields are small and every centimetre is farmed.

We found when we walked along Devil's Ditch that there were a lot of chalk stones.

Well you would, that is chalk rock. It is porous; that means that it allows water to soak into it. There are no streams here.

So the chalk rock forms the hills.

Yes, some of it is quite hard. It was quarried here and used for building.

We saw a lot of grain crops.

Yes it has been ploughed and by using fertilisers barley and wheat can be grown. Did you notice how large the fields were?

Large fields allow the machinery to be used easily.

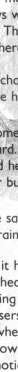

Reach: an inland port

The port where barges were unloaded.
They brought coal, timber, wine, salt and bricks.
They took stone, cloth, shoes and grain.

Roman canal now used for leisure boats

Reach Lode

Fen edge

The Hythe

Basin

Basin

N

Fen edge

West Reach

Fair green

East Reach

Quarries

The disused quarries from which the stone known as clunch was taken to build the houses.

Devil's Dyke

Devil's Ditch flattened in medieval times to make a place where a fair could be held

An ancient ditch and bank marking the boundary between two kingdoms

0 —— 100 metres
0 —— 100 yards

1 Copy and complete the labelling of the cross section of the walk using the following labels:
   Chalk land low hills – Drained marshland many ditches – No streams – Fertile soil growing vegetable and grain crops – Wheat and barley grown in large fields
2 Make a list of three reasons why the village grew at this point on the Fen edge.

3 Draw a framework like the one below and list all the differences you can find between the Fen and upland.

DIFFERENT LANDS

FEN	UPLAND

4 Look at the map of Reach.
(a) What evidence is there that Reach was once a port?
(b) What other evidence is there that the village was once more important that it is now?
5 Join with a friend. Make a list of places and features which might help to tell the story of the past in your home area.

Different Soils

When we took our walk we noticed that the soils on the Fen were different to the soils on the chalk.

Well, there are quite a lot of ways of finding the differences between soils. Farms and gardeners need to know all about soil to grow the best crops.

Yes. Our problem was we didn't know how they were different.

First you need to know what soil is made of. Look through the microscope.

Soil through the microscope

Peat soil blowing

WATER — fills many spaces between particles. Needed for plants to absorb the minerals in the water.

HUMUS — rotted vegetation. Provides materials which plants need to be able to grow.

ROCK — pieces of the underlying rock, provide minerals for plants to be able to grow.

AIR — between particles, allows the animals which live in the soil to breathe.

Soil can be tested for:
- acidity
- depth
- texture

Acidity

Different plants like different soils in which to grow. Some plants like acid soils such as peat, others less acid soils like chalk. Most plants like neutral soils.

We can test how acid a soil is by finding its PH value. If the number is above 7.0 the soil is **alkaline** or less acid. If the number is below 6.0 then the soil is acid. Farmers can change the acid level by using chemicals and fertilisers.

Finding Acidity

Take a test tube and into it put
- 3 cm of soil
- Distilled water ⅔ way up the tube
- 2 cm of barium sulphate powder
- A few drops of soil indicator.
Place the cork on top of the tube and shake.
Allow to settle and check colour against chart to find the PH value.

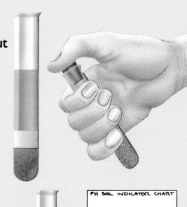

Depth

Look for a ditch or hole which shows the soil and the rock underneath. You will see three layers:

Dark soil – fertile layer

Light soil – less fertile

Rock

The dark humus layer is very important. A deep humus layer will help plants grow well.

Texture

Soils have a different 'feel' or texture. This depends on the rock particles in the soil.

The soil may be:

SANDY SOIL

This will feel sandy and gritty. There will be little humus. The soil will be dry. It is very easy to work.

CLAY SOIL

This will feel smooth and sticky when wet. When wet it can easily be rolled into a ball. It is difficult to work as it is sticky when wet and hard when dry.

LOAM

This clings to the hand and is silky to 'feel'. It contains humus and holds just the right amount of water. It is easy to work.

SOIL CAN BE: SANDY — SANDY LOAM — LOAM — CLAYEY LOAM — CLAY

Different Soils

FEN SOIL		CHALK SOIL
PH 5.5 ← ACIDITY → PH 7.5		
Acid		Alkaline
Deep soil	← DEPTH →	Shallow soil
Very light soil no grit or stones	← TEXTURE →	Light gritty with stones

Peat soil

The fen soil is peat. It is black, with a lot of humus and is very fertile. As the marsh of the fen was drained the peat shrank and the land became lower. Reach Lode is now higher than the land. The soil is very light and blows away. We are beginning now to plough up the clay beneath.

The peat fen soil is acid. It is good for growing carrots, oats, potatoes and celery.

The chalk soil is alkaline. It is a very thin soil and does not contain much humus. With the use of fertilisers however, farmers can grow barley and wheat year after year in the same fields.

1 Draw two diagrams like the ones below and label the differences between chalk and peat soil.

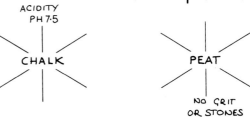

ACIDITY
PH 7.5

CHALK

PEAT

NO GRIT OR STONES

2 Try a soil test on the soil at home or at school.

A Part of East Anglia?

"We are told that Reach is a part of the region called East Anglia. But we are not sure what East Anglia means, so we tried to find out."

"We found that there were many different ideas. Some people suggested the boundary is the edge of the higher land to the west and to the south."

"We looked at maps of the United Kingdom to see what was the same in East Anglia and what was different from the rest of the country."

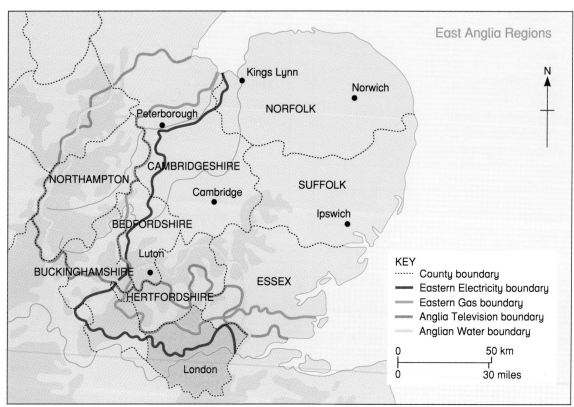

East Anglia Regions

N

Kings Lynn

Norwich

NORFOLK

Peterborough

CAMBRIDGESHIRE

NORTHAMPTON

SUFFOLK

Cambridge

Ipswich

BEDFORDSHIRE

Luton

BUCKINGHAMSHIRE

ESSEX

HERTFORDSHIRE

London

KEY
.... County boundary
—— Eastern Electricity boundary
—— Eastern Gas boundary
—— Anglia Television boundary
—— Anglian Water boundary

| 0 | | 50 km |
| 0 | | 30 miles |

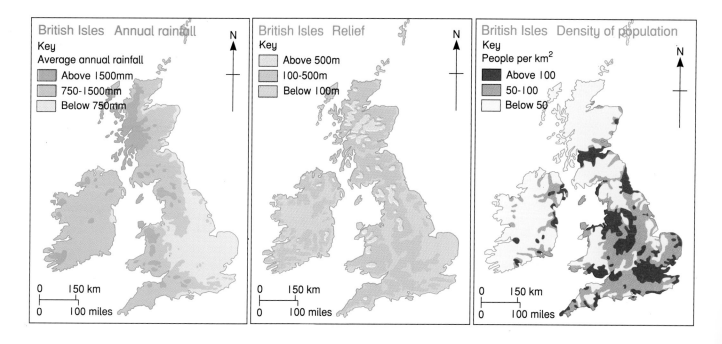

British Isles   Annual rainfall

N

Key
Average annual rainfall
Above 1500mm
750-1500mm
Below 750mm

0   150 km
0   100 miles

British Isles   Relief

N

Key
Above 500m
100-500m
Below 100m

0   150 km
0   100 miles

British Isles   Density of population

N

Key
People per km^2
Above 100
50-100
Below 50

0   150 km
0   100 miles

A Breckland heath and forest

C The Broadland

B Agricultural rolling chalk landscape

D Flat Fenland

Map labels: Broadland, Fenland, C, D, B Chalk/clay farmland, A, Breckland

1 (a) Make a tracing of the coast outline of East Anglia from the map 'East Anglia Regions'.
(b) Draw the boundary of what you think is East Anglia.
(c) Use your atlas to mark on your map – four inland towns
    – four coastal towns
    – the names of the counties
    – four rivers.
2 Use the evidence from the maps to write down the correct word from the brackets in the following:
(a) The population density in East Anglia is (high/low/mixed).
(b) East Anglia as a whole has a (high/low) rainfall.

(c) East Anglia is a (low lying/highland) area.
3 (a) A region should have sameness about it. Copy the table below. Tick the boxes according to whether East Anglia has sameness or not for the features listed.

IS EAST ANGLIA A REGION?		
FEATURES	SAMENESS	NOT SAME
1. Relief		
2. Rainfall		
3. Density of population		
4. Landscapes		
5. Service areas		

(b) From the evidence on this page and your table, do you think East Anglia is a region? Write two sentences giving reasons for your answer.

Working in East Anglia

" What changes are taking place in the work of the people in East Anglia? "

" In Reach we found a change. Instead of most people working in farming, many now work in the towns and cities. People from Cambridge have bought houses in the village and drive to Cambridge to work each day.
Where several men were needed to harvest in the past, large machines and one man will do their work today. "

East Anglian farming scene – drilling sugar beet

Manor Farm: an East Anglian arable farm

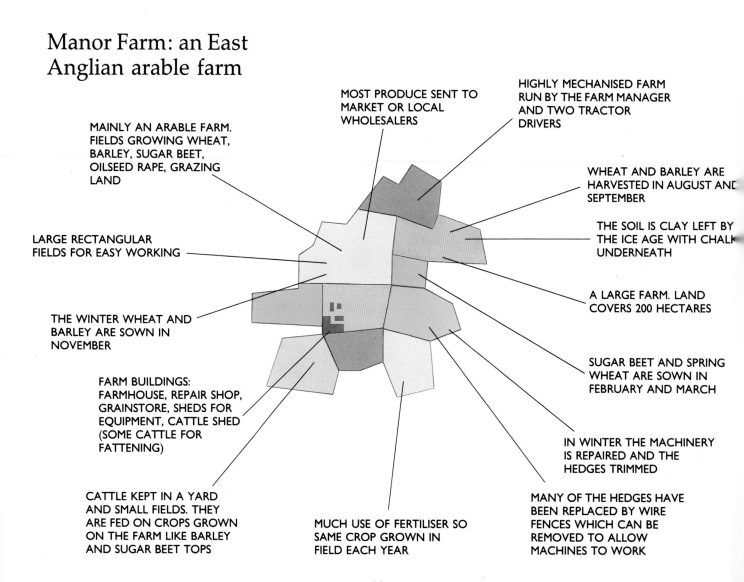

MOST PRODUCE SENT TO MARKET OR LOCAL WHOLESALERS

HIGHLY MECHANISED FARM RUN BY THE FARM MANAGER AND TWO TRACTOR DRIVERS

MAINLY AN ARABLE FARM. FIELDS GROWING WHEAT, BARLEY, SUGAR BEET, OILSEED RAPE, GRAZING LAND

WHEAT AND BARLEY ARE HARVESTED IN AUGUST AND SEPTEMBER

THE SOIL IS CLAY LEFT BY THE ICE AGE WITH CHALK UNDERNEATH

LARGE RECTANGULAR FIELDS FOR EASY WORKING

A LARGE FARM. LAND COVERS 200 HECTARES

THE WINTER WHEAT AND BARLEY ARE SOWN IN NOVEMBER

SUGAR BEET AND SPRING WHEAT ARE SOWN IN FEBRUARY AND MARCH

FARM BUILDINGS: FARMHOUSE, REPAIR SHOP, GRAINSTORE, SHEDS FOR EQUIPMENT, CATTLE SHED (SOME CATTLE FOR FATTENING)

IN WINTER THE MACHINERY IS REPAIRED AND THE HEDGES TRIMMED

CATTLE KEPT IN A YARD AND SMALL FIELDS. THEY ARE FED ON CROPS GROWN ON THE FARM LIKE BARLEY AND SUGAR BEET TOPS

MUCH USE OF FERTILISER SO SAME CROP GROWN IN FIELD EACH YEAR

MANY OF THE HEDGES HAVE BEEN REPLACED BY WIRE FENCES WHICH CAN BE REMOVED TO ALLOW MACHINES TO WORK

Employment changes in East Anglia

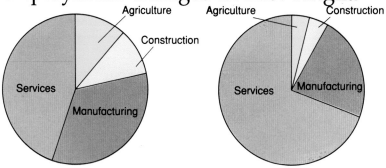

1960

1990

New industry in East Anglia

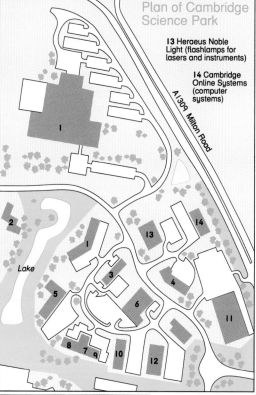

1 Napp Pharmaceutical Group (research and preparation of medicines)

2 Nickerson International Seed (plant breeding)

3 Signal Processors (electronic signal processing systems)

4 Nokia-Mobira (cellular radio telephone systems)

5 Cambridge Life Sciences (diagnostic systems for veterinary health care)

6 Design Computions (design software for architects and draughtsmen)

7 DLB Systems (suppliers of software to the pharmaceutical industry)

8 Agricultural Genetics (plant biotechnology genetic engineering and tissue culture)

9 PAFRA (low temperature preservation of biological material)

10 Napp Pharmaceutical Group

11 Laserscan (digital mapping and geographical information graphics engineering)

12 Vaisala (UK) (development and manufacture of meteorological instruments and systems)

Plan of Cambridge Science Park

13 Heraeus Noble Light (flashlamps for lasers and instruments)

14 Cambridge Online Systems (computer systems)

A1309 Milton Road

Lake

Many changes are taking place in the jobs people do in East Anglia. New industries have grown up on estates on the edge of towns. The best known of these estates is the Cambridge Science Park.

Trinity College owned an area of land on the northern outskirts of Cambridge. The land was flat. It was separated from **residential** areas, was on the A45 northern bypass and was close to the M11. Any new industry could make links with research carried out at Cambridge University.

Officially opened in 1975, there are now 81 industries at the Science Park. They make instruments, computers, lasers, vaccines and provide scientific services to industry.

High technology factories in Cambridge Science Park

1 Copy the table below. Use the information about Manor Farm to complete the gaps in the table.

MANOR FARM – EAST ANGLIA
Type of farm:-
Size of farm:-
Number of workers:-
Soil:-
Crops grown:-
Animals kept:-

2 Use the pie charts to list two changes that have taken place in working in East Anglia between 1960 and 1990.
3 Use the map of the Industrial Estate near Cambridge to list the types of industry found there.
4 Why do you think this industrial estate is called a Science Park?
5 Would you rather work on a farm or in a factory like those shown? Give a reason for your answer.

Living and Moving in East Anglia

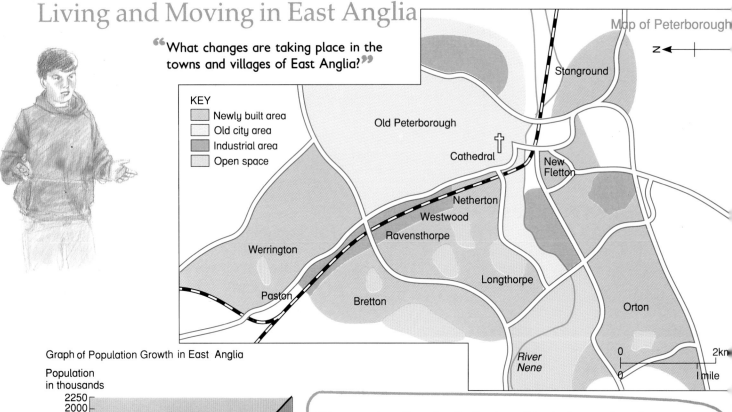

Map of Peterborough

“What changes are taking place in the towns and villages of East Anglia?”

KEY
- Newly built area
- Old city area
- Industrial area
- Open space

Stanground

Old Peterborough

Cathedral

New Fletton

Netherton

Westwood

Ravensthorpe

Werrington

Longthorpe

Paston

Bretton

Orton

River Nene

0   2km
0   1mile

Graph of Population Growth in East Anglia

Population in thousands

2250
2000
1750
1500
1250
1000
750
500
250
0

1801   1851   1901   1951   1991

We moved to East Anglia for its peace and quiet. I am a designer and my husband is a teacher and found a job here. We moved to Norfolk to this cottage five years ago. We sold our house in Birmingham to buy the cottage. It needed a lot of repairs. We got a local builder to do the improvements. We like the peace and quiet of village life.

1 Look at the map of Peterborough.
Copy and fill in the blanks in the following using some of the words below (there are more than you need).

CHANGES IN PETERBOROUGH
Three of the new housing areas which have been built are called ____ ____ and ____ . New main roads have been built ____ housing areas. Open space has been left ____ the housing area. The new areas growing around Peterborough will almost __ __ its size.

CASTOR   DOUBLE   THROUGH   TRIPLE
NEAR TO   ORTON   BRETTON   WITHIN   PASTON
ROUND THE OUTSIDE OF   AWAY FROM

2 Use the evidence from this page to make a list of reasons why people would wish to move from London to Peterborough.

We moved to East Anglia from the East End of London. Our house there was very old and damp. In Peterborough we have a nice new house on the Bretton estate. There is more room, nice parks, and my husband has a job in the Bretton industrial area. He used to work in the docks. We miss London's bustle and life but I wouldn't go back to live there.

"What changes are taking place in transport in East Anglia?"

Local Bus Service

Swaffham Circular
via Foulden & Gt. Cressingham
by Freedom Travel

All stops on route will be recognised and in rural areas the service will operate a Hail and Ride. The service is now subsidised by Norfolk County Council

Fridays only

Swaffham, Market Place	0935
Cockley Cley, Bus Shelter	0945
Gooderstone, Swan	0952
Oxborough, Church	0956
Foulden, Walnut Close	1000
Foulden, Vicarage Close	1003
Hilborough, Council Houses	1013
Hilborough, Post Office	1015
Gt. Cressingham, Church	1023
Swaffham, Market Place	1038
Swaffham, Market Place	1405
Gt. Cressingham, Church	1420
Hilborough, Post Office	1428
Hilborough, Council Houses	1429
Foulden, Vicarage Close	1437
Foulden, Walnut Close	1439
Oxborough, Church	1444
Gooderstone, Swan	1448
Cockley Cley, Bus Shelter	1453
Swaffham, Market Place	1500

For Saturday service see over

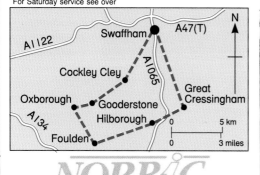

NORBiC

INTERCITY

Norwich and Yarmouth → London

InterCity train service 1 October 1990 to 12 May 1991
First Class and standard accommodation
Light food and hot and cold drinks
Reservable seats available

Mondays to Fridays

Great Yarmouth Depart	Norwich Depart	Liverpool Street Arrive
—	0500	0655
—	0530	0725
—	0600	0755
—	0635	0836
0620	0705	0900
0702	0745	0925
—	0805	0955
0816	0905	1050
0915	1005	1150
1020	1100	1250
1120	1200	1350
1215	1300	1450
1320	1400	1550
1420	1500	1650
1520	1600	1750
1600	1700	1853
1717	1800	1950
1805	1900	2055
1947	2030	2230

Saturdays

Great Yarmouth Depart	Norwich Depart	Liverpool Street Arrive
—	0500	0651
—	0600	0750
0620	0700	0850
0702	0800	0950
0702	0830	1025
0816	0900	1050
0851	0945	1145
0915	1000	1150
1020	1100	1250
—	1200	1350
1215	1300	1450
1320	1400	1550
1420	1500	1650
1520	1600	1750
1600	1700	1850
1717	1800	1950
1805	1900	2055
1825	2000	2155
2015	2100	2255

Sundays

Great Yarmouth Depart	Norwich Depart	Liverpool Street Arrive
0815	0900	1059
1016	1100	1259
1215	1300	1459
—	1400	1559
1400	1500	1659

Norwich – London train timetable

I live in Foulden. I do not drive. I have to rely on the Freedom Travel bus. The bus comes on two days of the week: Friday which is market day and Saturday. On each day there is only one bus to Swaffham in the morning and one bus back again in the afternoon.

3 Look at the Freedom Travel timetable for the journeys from Foulden to Swaffham on Fridays.

(a) At what time would you catch the bus in the morning from Walnut Close?

(b) At what time would you arrive in Swaffham?

(c) At what time would you leave Swaffham?

(d) At what time would you arrive home at Walnut Close?

(e) How long would the journey take?

(f) How long would you have to spend shopping in Swaffham?

4 Look at the Intercity railway timetable from Norwich to London on Mondays to Fridays.

(a) How many trains run each day from Norwich to London?

(b) If you caught the 0905 at what time would you arrive in London?

(c) How long would the journey on the 0905 take from Norwich to London?

5 Join with a friend.

Make a list of the changes in 'Living and Moving in East Anglia' from the evidence on these pages. Decide whether you think the changes will be for the best for East Anglia.

The Heart of the Region – Norwich

Hospital

"Is there a place which can be called the
centre of the region?"

NORWICH
POPULATION –
121 600

Cathedral

Market

NORWICH –
MAIN
INDUSTRY
Food Processing
Communications
Shoe Manufacture
Insurance
Printing
Window Manufacture
Chemical Manufacture

NORWICH –
MAIN
INDUSTRY
Norwich Union
Anglia TV
Her Majesty's
    Stationery
    Office
May and Baker
Start-Rite
Reckitt and
    Colman
Anglian
    Windows

Elm Hill, near city centre

Theatre

"Norwich is a great heritage
city housing a remarkable collection of museums,
art galleries, historic buildings, and speciality shops
set amidst a medieval street pattern reserved for pedestrians."

Norwich – A History

Norwich has a history going back over 900 years.
When the Normans came to England in 1066 they
built a castle at Norwich. Today's castle stands on the
same site.

Nearby, about 30 years later, Bishop de Losinga
began the building of the Cathedral with a spire over
100 metres high.

Norwich was once the second city of England. The
large market served the surrounding area.

At first it was wool and weaving based on local
sheep farming which made Norwich rich. Then the
steam powered mills of northern England took the
trade. Norwich turned to shoes, mustard and other
industry based on the farm produce of the region.

SIZE OF TOWNS
Norwich   – 121 600
Ipswich   – 122 800
Cambridge   – 98 500
Peterborough   – 134 900
Kings Lynn   – 30 100
Great Yarmouth   – 50 100
Lowestoft   – 52 200
Bury St Edmunds – 25 600

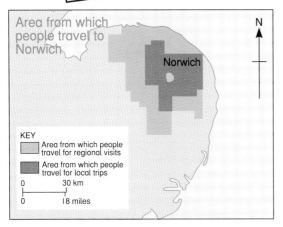

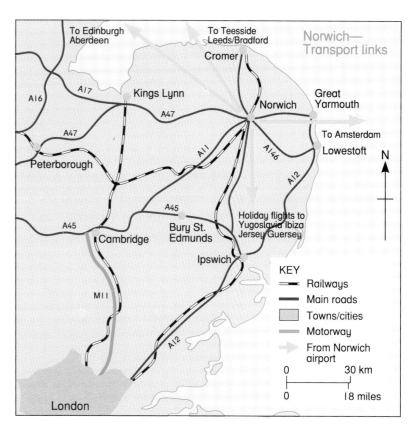

Visitors to Norwich

We come to Norwich shopping about once a month. We live in a village about 40 km (25 miles) away. We come to buy special things like clothes, furniture or jewellery.

I've come to Norwich to the planning office – my company is planning a new housing estate in a village nearby and we need to obtain planning permission.

We've come to spend a holiday in East Anglia and have come to see the historic sites of Norwich.

I travel about 30 km (19 miles) to Norwich each day to work.

I'm here in Norwich today to visit the theatre – I will go to the Castle Museum this afternoon.

1 Look at the photographs on page 16. Make a list of the things shown on the photographs which would attract people to Norwich.
2 Write out the two lists of NORWICH – MAIN INDUSTRY matching the name of the firm to the correct industry.
3 Which old industries are still found in Norwich?

4 Look at the table of SIZE OF TOWNS and the maps NORWICH – TRANSPORT LINKS, AREA FROM WHICH PEOPLE TRAVEL TO NORWICH, and the cartoon of VISITORS TO NORWICH. Join with a friend and
(a) Use this evidence to decide whether you think Norwich can be called 'The Heart of the Region'.
(b) Give as many reasons as you can for your answer.

THE OX LEE
FILE

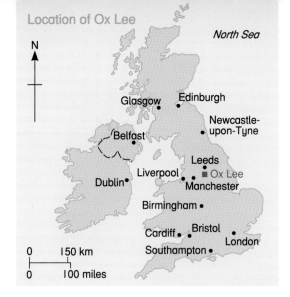

Location of Ox Lee

North Sea

N

Glasgow • Edinburgh

Newcastle-upon-Tyne •

Belfast

Leeds

Liverpool • ■ Ox Lee

Dublin • Manchester

Birmingham •

Cardiff • Bristol

Southampton • London

0   150 km

0   100 miles

Areas of beautiful landscape are very precious. So are **mineral resources** which we need to be able to live. Often these **resources** are found in beautiful areas. Then we must decide whether to mine or to leave the resources in the ground.

Ox Lee from Cheese Gate Nab

Environment Survey

	1	2	3	4	5	
UGLY						BEAUTIFUL
BORING						INTERESTING
NOISY						QUIET
SPOILT						UNSPOILT
POLLUTED						UNPOLLUTED
DULL						VARIED
DIRTY						CLEAN
ORDINARY						SPECTACULAR
UNTIDY						TIDY
HOSTILE						WELCOMING
TOTAL =						

‖ Look at the Environment Survey table and the photograph of Ox Lee. (The Environment Survey helps you to describe your surroundings.)

(a) Decide how you feel about the countryside in the photograph. To help you:

(i) On a copy of the table place a tick under the score you have chosen for each of the pairs of words.

(ii) Add up your final score. What does this tell you about your feelings for the countryside at Ox Lee?

(b) Compare your scores with others in the class. Are they similar? If not, why not?

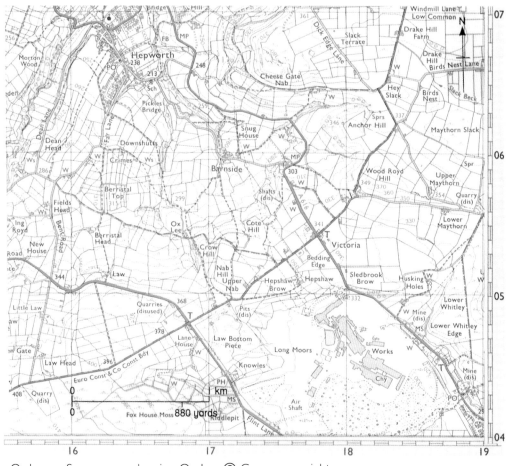

Ordnance Survey map showing Ox Lee © Crown copyright

'Last of the Summer Wine' Country

The derelict farm of Ox Lee lies on a hillside three kilometres south of Holmfirth. It is here that the famous television series 'Last of the Summer Wine' is filmed. The local tourist office is working hard to use the interest in the television series to attract visitors to the area. A local bus company runs coach trips giving people the chance to enjoy the 'summer wine' countryside in comfort.

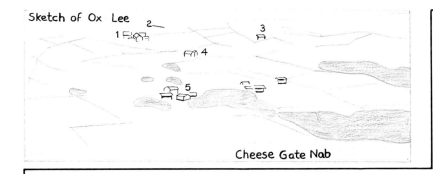

Sketch of Ox Lee

Cheese Gate Nab

2 Look at the map, sketch and photograph which was taken from Cheese Gate Nab (grid reference 175 066).

(a) Make a list of numbers 1 to 5 and next to each give the correct name of the feature shown on the sketch. Choose from this list of names:

  HEPSHAW BROW, BARNSIDE, VICTORIA,
  OX LEE, LAW.

(b) Make a list of evidence from the map of **manufacturing industry** in the area.

(c) Imagine that you were going to follow a route on footpaths and roads round the map. You are given the following grid references.

Ox Lee	168054	Barnside	172059
Lane House	168048	Fields Head	159056
Cheese Gate Nab	175066	Hepworth	164066

Plan your route and then:

(i) list the grid references in the order you would pass through them

(ii) name six features you would pass on your route in the order you would pass them

(iii) write down the height of the highest point on your route.

A Quarry at Ox Lee

The derelict (disused) farm at Ox Lee is owned by Hepworth Clay Products. In December 1988 the firm applied to Kirklees Council for permission to develop a 28 hectare quarry at the farm.

History of the Farm

Hepworths have been in the area since 1860. In those days the firm was the Hepworth Iron Company, one of the many small iron works using the local iron ore and coal of the area. By 1900 the company was making use of the very pure clay found beneath the coal to make clay pipes.

In 1970 the company became Hepworth Building Products. They built a revolutionary new kiln. The company now makes 80% of all the clay pipes manufactured in Britain.

The Product

The Hepworth pipes are strong and long lasting. They rely on a mixture of clays, one of which is known as Halifax Hard Bed clay. This clay is only found in the area local to the firm and is present at Ox Lee. The pipes are mainly used for drainage.

Hepworth's Hazlehead works

The Proposal

Hepworth Building Products asked for permission to quarry Halifax Hard Bed clay at Ox Lee Farm. The quarry would eat into the hillside to a depth of 35 metres. The clay would then be transported by lorry on a new road up a 1 in 10 (10%) hill to the works. The clay would be quarried in strips. Each strip would be filled in as the next strip was opened.

Quarrying at Ox Lee would last 20 years. After the work is finished the land would be returned as it was before quarrying started.

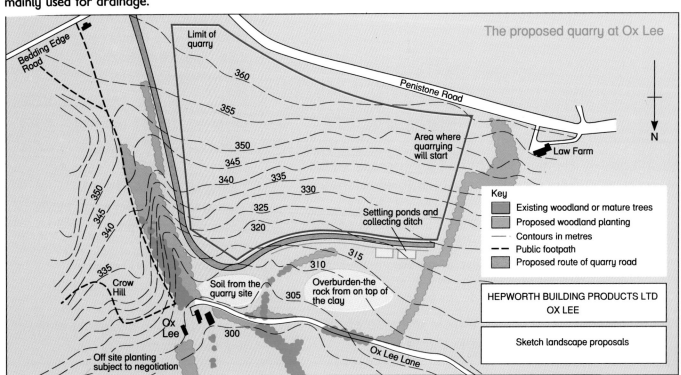

The proposed quarry at Ox Lee

Key
- Existing woodland or mature trees
- Proposed woodland planting
- Contours in metres
- Public footpath
- Proposed route of quarry road

HEPWORTH BUILDING PRODUCTS LTD
OX LEE

Sketch landscape proposals

20

- **Why do you need to quarry at Ox Lee?**
  We built a £1.5 million kiln to make high quality pipes. This new technology is why today we are the leading manufacturer. For high quality pipes we need Halifax Hard Bed clay from Ox Lee.

- **Why at Ox Lee; is there nowhere else?**
  We had a request turned down at a site overlooking the Peak District National Park. Our other quarries are running out of clay. Ox Lee is the only site and it is near our works.

- **Won't it damage the beauty of this area?**
  There will be some effect on the environment. We will hide the site with trees. This site faces north and is usually in shadow so will not be noticed. Few homes directly overlook the site.

- **How important is the quarry to this firm?**
  We employ almost 1 000 local people. We would not wish to stop pipe making at Hepworth.

- **What will happen to the site when the clay has been quarried?**
  We will of course restore the landscape. You will not know a quarry was ever there.

LOCAL NEWSPAPER
REPORTER

COMPANY
SPOKESPERSON

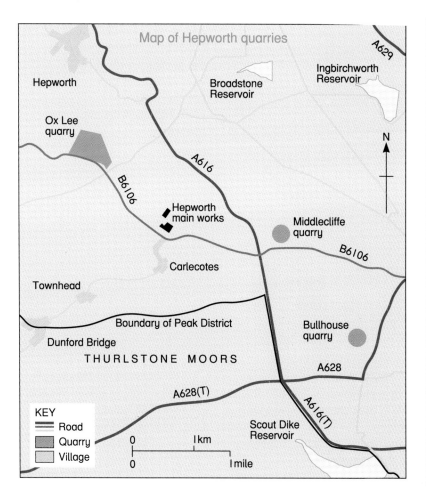

Map of Hepworth quarries

KEY
- Road
- Quarry
- Village

0   1 km
0   1 mile

1 (a) Draw a diagram like the one below.
(b) There are many different reasons why Hepworths should quarry for clay at Ox Lee. Use the evidence on this page to write one reason in each bubble.

Few houses overlook the site

A QUARRY AT OX LEE

On the Other Side of the Fence

Ox Lee quarry site

Overburden
piled on site

Ber

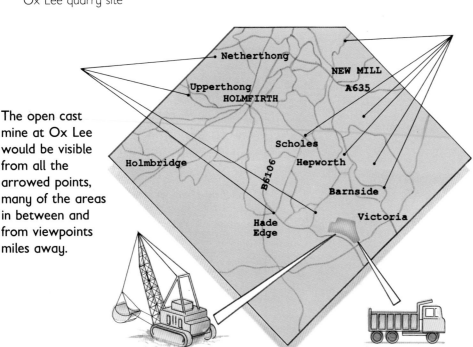

The open cast mine at Ox Lee would be visible from all the arrowed points, many of the areas in between and from viewpoints miles away.

People use all the footpaths shown, and many others. From all of them the walkers will hear the noise and see the ugly workings spoiling the view.

What it means!

To mine the land at Ox Lee the firm must remove 100 feet of **overburden** (the rock on top of the clay) to get at a mineral known locally as Halifax Hard Bed clay. The company uses this to help them to make clay pipes at the Hazlehead factory.

Work will go on for twenty years – it will make spoil heaps, noise and disturbance. It will ruin the peace and quiet of the footpaths and the landscape in the surrounding area.

The company's two quarries at Middlecliffe and Bullhouse show the sort of effect mineral working at Ox Lee would have.

Bulldozers, heavy lorries, a dragline and other equipment would be used.

Is It Necessary?

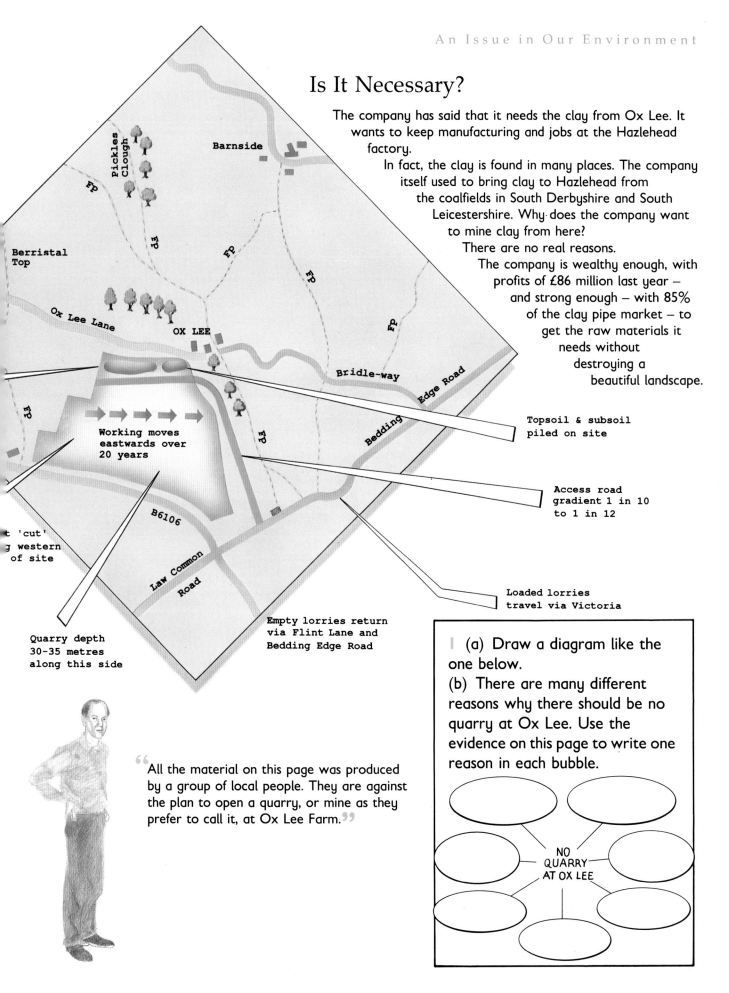

Pickles Clough

Barnside

FP

FP

FP

Berristal Top

FP

Ox Lee Lane

OX LEE

FP

Bridle-way

Edge Road

Bedding

Working moves eastwards over 20 years

FP

B6106

t 'cut' g western of site

Law Common Road

Quarry depth 30-35 metres along this side

Empty lorries return via Flint Lane and Bedding Edge Road

Topsoil & subsoil piled on site

Access road gradient 1 in 10 to 1 in 12

Loaded lorries travel via Victoria

The company has said that it needs the clay from Ox Lee. It wants to keep manufacturing and jobs at the Hazlehead factory.

In fact, the clay is found in many places. The company itself used to bring clay to Hazlehead from the coalfields in South Derbyshire and South Leicestershire. Why does the company want to mine clay from here?

There are no real reasons.

The company is wealthy enough, with profits of £86 million last year – and strong enough – with 85% of the clay pipe market – to get the raw materials it needs without destroying a beautiful landscape.

"All the material on this page was produced by a group of local people. They are against the plan to open a quarry, or mine as they prefer to call it, at Ox Lee Farm."

l (a) Draw a diagram like the one below.
(b) There are many different reasons why there should be no quarry at Ox Lee. Use the evidence on this page to write one reason in each bubble.

NO QUARRY AT OX LEE

The Campaign

Dateline Ox Lee

The campaigners

8th Feb
A meeting of local people held in the Hepworth Village Hall. A person from the company answers questions

5th Feb
60 people who live nearby walk round the quarry site - action group formed

20-21st Jan
Local newspapers carry reports and photographs of the plans

25th Nov
First notice of the quarry in the local newspaper

20th Jan
Hepworth Clay Products hold an exhibition explaining the quarry at Holmfirth Civic Hall

Feb to March
Action group make contact with local planners

9th March
A public meeting held at Hepworth Village Hall with a chance to hear and question local councillors

14th May
Action group visit British Geological Survey in Nottingham to obtain the facts

20th June
LETTER received from local Member of Parliament from the House of Commons giving support for the Action Group

Dec to Nov
Letter sent to local newspapers

July to Nov
Action Group talk to councillors

Nov
Special meeting of the Planning Sub-Committee to decide the case

| NOV | DEC | JAN | FEB | MARCH | APRIL | MAY | JUNE | JULY | AUG | SEPT | OCT | NOV |

1988

1989

---

9 February 1989

QUARRY BENEFITS

C. M. Main Street, Hepworth.

I was very disappointed that some people are against the quarry at Ox Lee.

The company badly needs the clay to stay in business. If they cannot open this quarry then jobs may be lost.

The land being used is almost useless. Also the ruined hamlet of Ox Lee will be rebuilt when the site is returned at the end of quarrying.

I am sure those who wish to find peaceful walks will find many of them nearby whilst the quarrying is taking place.

I worked for the company for 50 years. It has brought wealth to the area since 1858. I say allow the quarry and let us all benefit from this go-ahead company.

16 February 1989

GROUNDS FOR LOCAL CONCERN

A. B. High Street, Hepworth.

I am sorry that C. M. of Main Street does not understand the worry many of us have about the Ox Lee Quarry. It will be a blot on the land for 20 years.

The land at Ox Lee is far from useless. It is part of the area in which tourism is being developed by the Council. Surely even C. M. can see that such a large quarry will be seen for many miles and spoil this beauty.

Is this quarry really needed? All our evidence tells us that we don't know. We don't want to put jobs at risk. But surely we need the answer to this question.

The Decision

One of the campaigners takes a final walk at Ox Lee – quarrying will last 20 years

Quarry application passed

Kirklees Council Planning Sub-Committee decided to allow Hepworth Clay Products to open a quarry at Ox Lee. The local residents opposed to the scheme lost their case. The application was passed by just two votes.

Was it all worth it?

The Action Group felt that their campaign was worthwhile. They learned a lot, became firm friends with people they had never met before, but above all won orders for 65 conditions on the quarrying. These included an agreement that money would be guaranteed by the Company and the Council for restoring the site.

1 Look at 'Dateline Ox Lee'.
(a) How long did the campaign last?
(b) List four ways in which the Action Group kept the campaign alive during this time.
(c) (i) Letters were sent to the local newspaper throughout the campaign.
   If you were involved when would you have sent a letter to the newspaper?
 (ii) The Action Group decided to send a letter to the Secretary of State for the Environment. Which would you think would be the best month of the Campaign to send this letter?

EITHER
2 (a) What is the purpose of letters to the newspapers in a dispute of this kind?
(b) Decide whether you are for or against the proposal to open a quarry at Ox Lee.
Write a letter to the Planning Sub-Committee putting your point of view and the reasons for your viewpoint.

OR

3 (a) Imagine that you are members of the Planning Sub-Committee. Your task is to accept or reject the planning application at Ox Lee.
(b) Using evidence from this unit discuss whether you would allow this quarry at Ox Lee or not.
(c) Elect a spokesperson or as a group, report your decision to the whole class. Give full reasons for that decision.

Location of Carmarthen and Lynmouth

unit 3

RISING DAMP

H ere we look at why rivers flood. We look at the ways people cope with floods and the effects floods have on their lives.

Flood devastation Lynmouth 1952

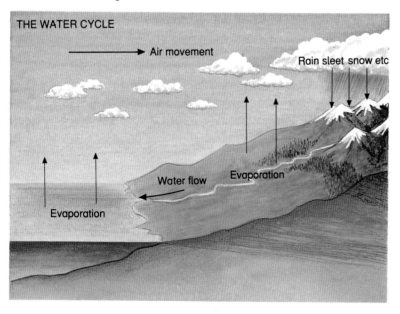

THE WATER CYCLE

What is a Flood?

Floods occur for many reasons. The most common is when too much rainwater flows into rivers. To understand why rivers flood, we need to look at how water reaches us. It reaches us because of the water or hydrological cycle, as it is called.

This describes how water moves over the earth, through the earth and through the atmosphere to affect us.

---

1 Make a large copy of the diagram of the water cycle. Add the labels and descriptions of the parts, from the list below, in the correct places.
2 Explain why you think it is called a 'cycle'.
3 Try to describe a smaller water cycle in your home or school.

Parts of the water cycle

PRECIPITATION – rain, sleet, hail, snow.
EVAPORATION – water being taken up, back into the atmosphere.
OVERLAND FLOW – water flowing across the land surface.
STREAMFLOW – water flowing in rivers or streams, ending up in the sea.
GROUNDWATER FLOW – water flowing underground, through the rock.
THROUGHFLOW – water flowing through the soil.
WATER TABLE – the upper level of saturated ground.

The Lynmouth Flood

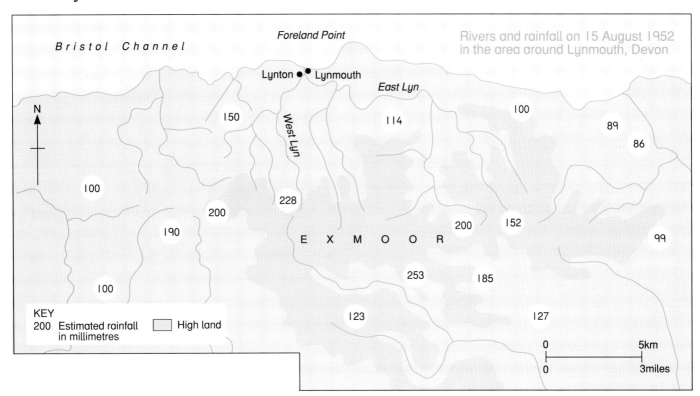

Bristol Channel

Foreland Point

Rivers and rainfall on 15 August 1952 in the area around Lynmouth, Devon

Lynton ● ● Lynmouth

East Lyn

West Lyn

N

150

114

100

89

86

100

228

200

152

190

E X M O O R

200

99

253

185

100

123

127

KEY
200 Estimated rainfall in millimetres   High land

0   5km
0   3miles

Lynmouth, in Devon, had a major flood in 1952. In the first two weeks of August, rain fell almost non-stop. Water washed into the rivers from the Exmoor highland. In the end the rivers flooded, ruining Lynmouth.

4 (a) Make a copy of the map.
(b) Label the following:-
TRIBUTARY – small stream joining the main river.
MOUTH – point where river ends, usually by flowing into the sea.
CATCHMENT AREA – area of streams and tributaries feeding a river.
5 Draw around the catchment area of the West Lyn and East Lyn rivers.
6 Why do you think the size of the catchment area was an important influence on the flooding?

Some of the press headlines

Biggest danger is peak tide

The wreckage of a town lies strewn across its beach

LITTLE STREAMS TURN KILLERS

Gifts, Large And Small, Swell Fund

TROOPS OUT IN 250 SQUARE MILES FLOOD AREA

120,000 TONS OF DEBRIS THREAT TO LYNMOUTH

Appeal made for 100 caravans

Firemen saved 14 from water

Flood town faces disaster

Community spirit shown in West flood area

AS the known death-rate in the Devon flood disaster rose last night, rain continued to fall and the sky was black.

HOTELS, HOUSES, CARS SWEPT AWAY

Why Did it Happen?

August, 1952 had been an exceptionally wet month on Exmoor. The soil was saturated. But if the rain had stopped, maybe it would have dried out. On Friday August 15th, there was no easing of the downpour. At 8.30pm there was a cloudburst! More than three months' worth of rain fell in 24 hours! Small streams became large ones, then burst their banks completely. Large trees and boulders were swept along with them. Stone bridges became filled with trees, boulders and telegraph poles. The torrent raced onwards at a speed of 20 km per hour. When the waters of the West Lyn and the East Lyn reached Lynmouth, everything was to be smashed before them. Waters hit Lynmouth as if through two funnels, from opposite directions!

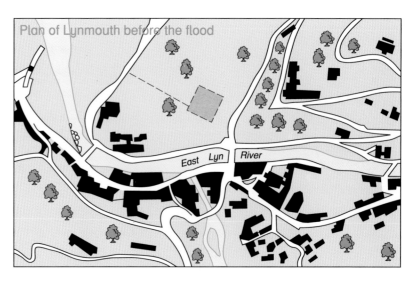

Plan of Lynmouth before the flood

East Lyn River

Lynmouth after the flood

East Lyn River

Riverside Road

West Lyn River

Flood protection measure at Lynmouth

Protection measures

Part of the Thames Barrier

1 ACCEPTING THE LOSS
This often happens in countries which can't afford to protect against flooding.

2 PUBLIC RELIEF MONEY
A fund may be set up after a disaster. For example, after the Lynmouth flood £1 300 000 had been collected by the summer of 1953.

3 FLOOD INSURANCE
Many people living in flood areas can insure their property against flood damage.

4 FORECASTING AND WARNING AGAINST FLOOD
Levels on the rivers can be looked at to give the public a warning about possible flooding. The media or police loud hailers or sirens can be used to warn communities against flooding.

5 RESERVOIRS
These can be built in the upper parts of rivers to store water to prevent sudden flooding.

6 MAKING THE CHANNEL LARGER
A river can be made deeper or wider, to hold more water before it overflows.

7 BANKS
Towns can be protected by walls or banks built on either side of the river. They are common because they are quite cheap. Flood relief channels are artificial channels which can be built to take away surplus water and prevent flooding.

8 BARRAGES
A dam or barrage can be built across a river to protect a community from flooding. This has happened on the River Thames, but is expensive.

9 FLOOD PLAIN ZONING
Land near to the river in the flood zone, called the flood plain, can be protected from certain sorts of land use or building.

Use an atlas to find maps of population distribution and rainfall of the British Isles (or look at the maps on page 10).

1 Which parts of the country receive the most rainfall?
2 Which areas are most densely populated?
3 Which areas therefore are most prone to flooding?
4 Why is this answer not the full story?
5 Spot the difference!
(a) How has Lynmouth changed as a result of the 1952 flood? List all the differences you can see between the maps.

(b) Describe changes in the river, the roads, the buildings and the land uses.
6 Look at the list of protection measures. Imagine you were living in Riverside Road. Produce a table, like the one below, to show the advantages and disadvantages of each method of protection.

Protection Method	Advantages	Disadvantages
Accept the loss	No costly building work	Solves nothing

Protection for Carmarthen

Carmarthen is on the River Towy. When large amounts of water flow in the river, and this happens at the same time as high tides, floods can result. After bad floods in 1979 and 1981, the Welsh Water Authority asked for a study to be made to prevent flooding. If the floods could not be stopped, ideas were needed to show how the effects could be lessened.

Flooding in Carmarthen

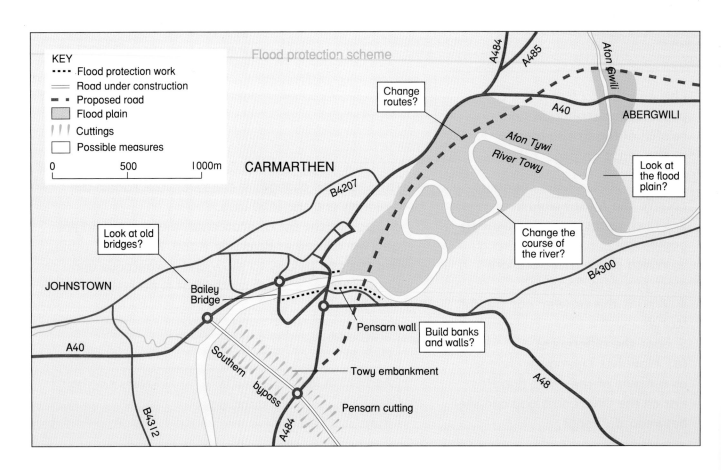

Flood protection scheme

KEY
- ····· Flood protection work
- ═ Road under construction
- ▬ ▬ Proposed road
- ▨ Flood plain
- ||| Cuttings
- ☐ Possible measures

0   500   1000m

CARMARTHEN

Change routes?

Afon Tywi
River Towy

ABERGWILI

Look at the flood plain?

Change the course of the river?

Look at old bridges?

JOHNSTOWN

Bailey Bridge

Pensarn wall

Build banks and walls?

Towy embankment

Southern bypass

Pensarn cutting

A40

B4312

A484

A48

B4300

B4207

A484   A485   Afon Gwili   A40

Preparing to Protect

The flood study carried out by the Welsh Water Authority tried to:-

- Collect information about flooding, for example river levels.
- Work out some solutions.
- Try and see what benefits these solutions may bring.

" You can build a small wall to protect against a little flood—one which returns every winter maybe. But it's the bigger floods that give us problems. Big ones may return every 10 years, but you'll need an expensive protection scheme to stop them. How often a flood returns is called its **return period.** "

How could this be done?

The floods in Carmarthen could perhaps have been stopped in a number of ways. These were the alternatives facing the 'flood protectors'. Many things were considered:-

- Information on water levels.
- Information on the flow of the river and the tides.
- Ways to develop the flood plain.
- Obstructions on the flood plain.
- Bridges on the river, and the types of bridge openings that were there.
- Places where flood prevention could be carried out.

What sort of action?

You represent Humphreys Engineers. Your firm is the one asked by the Welsh Water Authority to do the flood study.

You are keen to win the support of the people of Carmarthen for your project. They will be affected by whatever you decide.

1 Prepare a talk to a local secondary school, outlining your reasons for wanting to consider the points listed above.

2 Also, you need to think about the effects of any scheme you choose. Bring these points in to your talk:-

- removing bridges will alter the built environment
- raising the level of the flood plain changes the landscape
- dredging (removing silt from the river) will help the flow but cost money
- raising the flood wall will be an 'eyesore'.

River Towy: The Story of Flooding

All the places mentioned in the historic accounts are local to Carmarthen.

4 November 1931

The greatest flood within living knowledge was on Wednesday 4th when Carmarthen was completely isolated from road and rail traffic. The railway station was flooded almost to the platforms. A bus was practically submerged. Twelve houses were flooded completely in the main road. Traffic was held up throughout the area.

Report from the Carmarthen Journal of 15 November 1929:-
3–6 million tons of water passed under Carmarthen Bridge on Tuesday 12th. Rainfall on Monday 11th was 1.8 inches. The flood was the greatest for many years but higher levels had been reached when the tides were higher. Houses on the quay were flooded. Part of the village was under water. The whole valley was flooded. The greatest flood depth is recorded as 20.5 feet. On Tuesday the water level reached 19.4 feet.

Any flood protection scheme is worked out by thinking about how often the flood 'event' will happen. Small floods may happen about once every ten years for example. To stop these, perhaps by raising the height of a flood wall slightly, not much money need be spent. But once every 500 years, a major flood may occur. To prevent this, a lot of building has to be done, which costs a lot of money. This period in years, between which time no floods are likely, is called the return period.

Floods of 1933

Tides around this period were in the order of 17 feet. Flooding in Carmarthen resulted from this rather than any heavy rainfall. All the agricultural land in the valley was flooded.

SUMMARY OF ESTIMATED DAMAGE COSTS

Return Period (Years)	Carmarthen Quay (£s)
10	0
20	159 000
30	171 000
50	183 000
70	190 000
100	196 000
150	207 000
200	212 000
500	228 000

SUMMARY OF ESTIMATED COSTS OF PROTECTION

Return Period (Years)	Carmarthen Quay (£s)
20	110 000
30	125 000
50	144 000
70	156 000
100	172 000
150	189 000
200	200 000
500	231 000

1 Look at the historic accounts of flooding in Carmarthen. Draw a table showing:-

Causes of flooding in Carmarthen	Effects on the people of Carmarthen
11/11/29 1.8 inches of rain fell in the town	Flooding of houses on the quay

Complete the table.

2 (a) Draw a divided bar graph showing the estimated damage at Carmarthen Quay and the estimated cost of protection. Draw it in the way shown below.

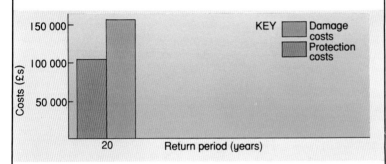

(b) After completing the graph explain why you think protection costs are usually lower than damage costs.

(c) What are the costs and benefits of choosing a large scheme for Carmarthen?

Flooding can cause damage in homes

Personal impacts

It is important to see how floods affect people. Mr Lewis, a resident, talks of some of the costs he has experienced.

"My name is Andrew Lewis. I live in the town and have to keep sandbags in my house to stop the flood waters. I have had four carpets ruined in the last 10 years. No insurance company will come near me. I'm sick with worry and have had a lot of time off work."

Cost of Protection

SOCIAL COSTS

Homes disturbed by building new constructions.

Traffic disrupted as bridge is closed.

Noise pollution as work is carried out.

River disturbed by dredging. Loss of an **amenity**.

ENVIRONMENTAL COSTS

Flood walls causing 'eyesores'.

Some buildings knocked down.

Landscape of flood plain changed.

Environmental impact of **pollution**.

Habitats changed in river and on banks.

3 Write a letter to the Town Council from Mr Lewis. Give your views on how he must feel.

unit 4

OUR CHANGING LIVES

NIGERIA

0 — 300 km
0 — 200 miles

Garoua

Ngaoundéré

Bamenda

Korup National Park

CAMEROON

Buea

Douala   Yaoundé

Atlantic Ocean

H ere we look at how people's lives are changing. Our study is of Cameroon, a tropical country in West Africa. The traditional village lifestyle, based on farming, is changing quickly. Industry is growing. More people are moving to the towns. The population is increasing quickly. More land is needed for these people and the **tropical rainforest** is under threat. Here we look into some of these issues.

My name is Hannah. My first language is French. I come from Douala, a French speaking industrial city. Most of the industries have strong links with France or are French firms. I have a place at the University of Yaoundé to read law. I hope to be a lawyer in Yaoundé, the seat of government and the capital city. French is also the spoken language in the capital and in government.

Our history is influenced by European countries. France, Germany and Britain all ruled part of Cameroon in the past. We were their **colonies**. They were the **colonisers**. The colonisers developed ports and main roads from the farms to the ports on the coast. They did this to take the crops grown to the ports, to **export** them. Exported crops were mainly bananas, oil-palm and rubber.

My name is Marcos and I am an English speaker. My home town is Kumba, which is in an English-speaking area which we call a province. The town gets little money from the government, and the roads are therefore poor. I have passed all my exams at school, but cannot get a place at university. This is because I do not speak French. Only a small number of places are given each year. The entrance exams are all in French.

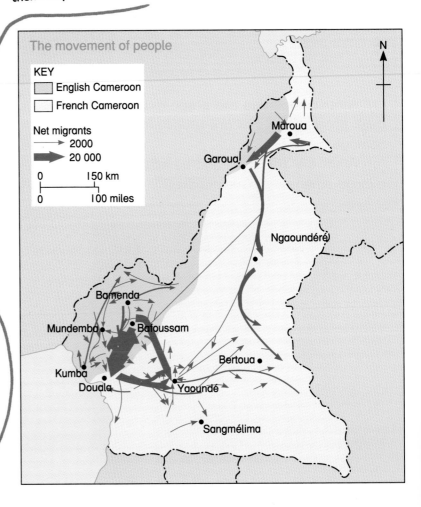

The movement of people

KEY

English Cameroon
French Cameroon

Net migrants
→ 2000
➡ 20 000

0 — 150 km
0 — 100 miles

Maroua

Garoua

Ngaoundéré

Bamenda

Mundemba   Bafoussam

Kumba

Douala   Yaoundé

Bertoua

Sangmélima

Plantations

Cameroon makes most of its money from the exports of oil palm. This is used in the West for products like soap (such as 'palm-olive'). Crops grown for selling overseas or export, such as palm oil and rubber, are usually grown on **plantations**. Look at the two photographs below. They are both taken in the south west province near Mundemba. One shows young oil palms and one shows a plantation which has been burnt. This was done by the owners after the palm was harvested.

The plantations are now often linked to industries in France. As you can see from the map many people wish to move into the French-speaking areas of Cameroon.

Oil palm plantation after burning

Young oil palm plantation

1 Why should the people move (or migrate) in this way, and not into the English-speaking areas?

2 Read the stories of Marcos and Hannah. Write down a list of positive and negative points about living in a country which was a colony.

3 From the two photos, describe what a plantation is like. Use the following questions to guide you.

(a) Are they owned by large businesses, by the government or by individual farmers? Why is this?

(b) Are they large or small? Why?

(c) Are palms planted in rows or in groups? Why?

(d) Is one crop grown or lots of crops?

(e) Are they near to or far from roads? Why?

4 Use the photos to describe the effects of a plantation on the landscape.

Markets Near and Far

Buea, a Market Town in Cameroon

Chesterfield Market

Buea Market

Cameroon Tribune No 1044, 10 August 1990

Kumba Market in Flames Again

Last Tuesday was a sad day for Kumba. The town woke up to find the market destroyed. This was the third fire in under two years. On 17 September 1988, 600 shops were burned and 1000 people lost their jobs. A month later, ten more shops burned down.

The cause of the fire on 7 August 1990 is unknown. How can the Council keep finding new homes and jobs for people? Tuesday's fire burned 66 shops. How did it happen? Who knows? The market attracted many visitors. Along with the Kumba Social Football Team, it was the main tourist attraction.

Fire spread by electricity cables. People were scared to get near them to put out the fire. If something isn't done soon, Kumba will be a ghost town.

1 Look at where crops are grown and animals are raised, on the maps opposite.
(a) Why do cash crops take up so much land?
(b) Suggest some uses for the animals kept.
2 Explain why certain crops are only sold and are not eaten or drunk within the country. Look at the two photographs of market scenes.
3 What differences can you see in the two markets?
4 Look at the produce sold and the ways in which it is displayed. Suggest why they are different.
5 Read the newspaper article 'Kumba Market in Flames Again'. Write down a list of the effects of the fire. Join with a friend and write a newspaper article for the local paper in Britain. This should describe the lives of a market trader in the tropics and one in Britain.

I work on a farm near Kumba. I cut bananas and send them to the **market**. The markets in my country have more functions than those in Britain. Our markets are our shops. There are no other shops, like yours. The markets in Buea and Kumba are our supermarkets, department stores and banks. So, when a disaster occurs such as a fire, we are ruined. Most products, or **cash crops**, are sold to the general public by our markets. Also, most people own little bits of land. On these they grow crops to be eaten by the family and not for sale. These are called **subsistence crops**.

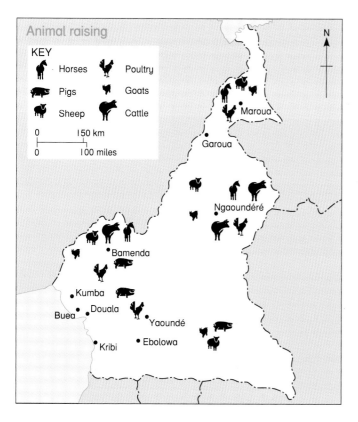

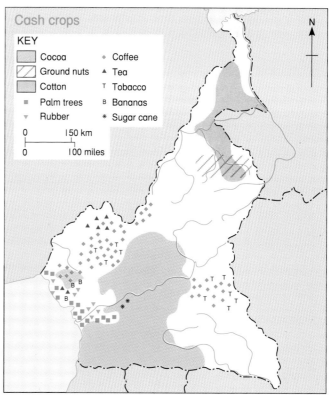

Changing Lifestyles

Cameroon is trying to protect its forests. This means it is trying to keep them for the future. Korup is one of Africa's oldest forests. It is Cameroon's first Tropical Rain Forest **National Park**. It is protected but still needs to be planned and looked after. The Park is the home for many villagers. Much of the land is used for subsistence farming. These people's lives are being affected by the ways the Park is looked after. The lines on the table show when the building will take place in the Park.

> "I teach in a secondary school in Kumba. Most children pay to come to school. There are more people now and much more money in the country. This is because money is earned by new industries and because resources such as oil are being developed. Most children can now afford to come to school. I have up to 150 in my class. I have little paper, no pens and no textbooks.
>
> Vandalism is on the increase. Classroom windows are often broken in the evenings. But standards of education and living standards are getting higher.
>
> More people are aware of the importance of the Korup Park. But, bad roads mean many people from Cameroon cannot get there. We have a plan for the Korup Park. I am teaching my children about these important conservation issues."

CHANGES PLANNED IN THE KORUP NATIONAL PARK

ACTIVITY	1989–90	1990–91	1991–92	1992–93	1993–94	1994–95
Build bridges and roads in park	———	———	———	———	———	———
Take air photos		———				
Map soils and plants			———			
Plan Mundemba-Toko road		———				
Build Mundemba-Toko road			———	———	———	
Agricultural development	———	———	———	———	———	———
Water, health, education provision	———	———	———	———	———	———
Resettle villagers	———	———	———	———	———	———

Bridge at entrance to Korup National Park

	Mean Monthly rainfall (mm)	Sunshine (hours) in the Korup Park
January	40	135
February	127	159
March	258	150
April	300	157
May	395	151
June	715	87
July	887	11
August	952	1
September	752	44
October	544	109
November	319	124
December	93	128

KEY
- ● Settlement
- — Main road
- Mangrove
- –·– National boundary
- Korup National Park (Cameroon)
- National Park (Nigeria)

0   30 km
0   18 miles

Look at the map and table 'Changes Planned in Korup Park'

1 Show the climate information above (either rainfall or sunshine) on a block graph.

2 You have been asked to produce a report for *GREENWATCH*, a local environmental paper near your school. They ask you to
(a) describe how the Korup Park might be managed (remember the different climatic conditions)
(b) say how local schools in Cameroon could be made more aware of rainforest issues.

39

All Change?

The changing lives in Cameroon are shown by these headlines. Changes are happening quickly. What are the effects?

Changes in Cameroon

The number of people in the country has grown, their lives have changed.

I work on the farms in Cameroon. The area I farm used to be rainforest. My mother could remember monkeys and other animals coming right up to the houses. Now, the men chase them for miles to hunt them. Their meat is sold at the side of the road. It is called 'bush meat'. My job is to look after the banana crop. Farm land is getting less and less. Towns are growing.

CAMEROON TRIBUNE

TUESDAY, MARCH 20, 1990   National Bi-weekly   No. 1003 PRICE : CFA 150

Street Maintenance Before Street Naming

Streets are still in poor repair. The government is considering giving all streets a name

After the 1990 World Cup Cameroon is football crazy. . .

LINKS WITH FRANCE INCREASE

The future of the port of Douala and that of Rouen in France will now be tied to each other following an agreement to twin up.

Anglo — Cameroon Friendship
Prince Charles is to visit the rainforest next month . . .

Express Mailing Now a Reality

US Donates Vehicles To Cameroon

The US assistance will boost health care services in the rural areas of the country . . .

Seeds For Sickle-Cell Treatment

Medical care is improving . . . .

Country	Population (thousands)	Average Density (per km²)	GNP Per Capita (US$) (Wealth per person)
USA	236 681	25	16 270
Japan	120 018	318	10 120
United Kingdon	55 624	228	8 970
France	54 935	100	10 400
West Germany	61 181	246	10 672
Switzerland	6 442	156	16 340
Zaire	32 084	14	160
Cameroon	9 467	20	834
Chad	4 901	4	59
Ethiopia	35 420	29	115
Nigeria	92 037	100	777

Figures from 1986

Douala and Kumba –
contrasting urban scenes

Growth of Total Population

Year	Population
1981	8 965 700
1982	9 205 200
1983	9 491 000
1984	9 790 900
1985	10 106 600
1986	10 446 400
1987	10 857 100
1988	11 180 600
1989	11 540 300
1990	11 899 600
1991	12 243 700

PROJECTION

Figures from 1985

1985	1990	1991 (forecast)
10 100 000	11 900 000	12 200 000

Table showing population change

POPULATION CHANGE IN CAMEROON

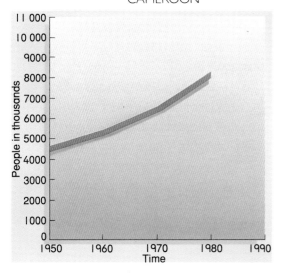

1 Make a table to show the good points and bad points of changes. Use the following headings down the side of your table.

HEALTH   TRANSPORT   TRADE LINKS   AID

2 Copy and complete the graph on population change in Cameroon.

3 Use the information given to find out about the population of Cameroon.

(a) What are the main changes in population in the country?

(b) How do you think they have affected Hannah's lifestyle?

4 (a) Describe three of the changes you have learnt about Cameroon.

(b) Share these with a partner and then discuss with another partner the most important changes in the country.

41

FROM HERE TO THERE

u n 5 *i t*

All of us make journeys. Some of us make daily journeys to school, to the shops or to work. We may go to the youth club, cinema, theatre or ice rink once a week or month. Longer journeys are made less often to go on holiday or a business conference. We all use different methods of transport but rely a great deal on our road and rail links. We seem to need more and more transport in Britain but which method should we use, road or rail? Which **route** do we take? How can we solve the traffic problems in our towns?

Location of Derbyshire

Camla's transport survey

Here are the journeys Camla makes in a week.
This is a radial chart. It shows her journeys in one week.
Answer the following questions using the chart.

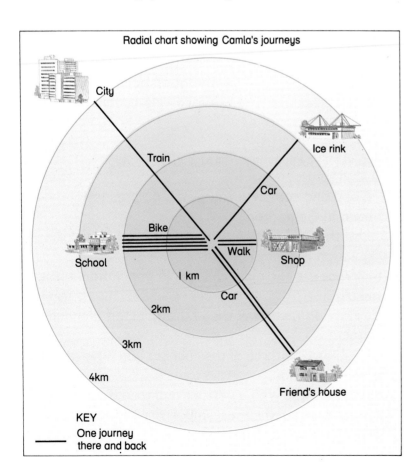

Radial chart showing Camla's journeys

KEY
——— One journey there and back

1 (a) Which journeys do I make most often?
(b) Which is the greatest distance I travelled and to where?
(c) How far have I travelled in one week?
(d) Look at the methods of transport I use. What can you say about the methods of transport I use and the distances I travel?
2 Draw a chart like this one to show your movements in a week. In what ways are your movements similar to mine?

42

"I go by bike to school. Pupils all over the world use different methods of transport. Some pupils go on a school bus. Others walk to school. Sometimes pupils go by train. In some parts of the world pupils may even fly to school. How do you go to school?"

"At school I made a survey of pupils in my class. I wanted to see where most pupils came from and how they travelled to school. Here are my results."

HOW DO YOU TRAVEL TO SCHOOL?

Bus	Walk	Car	Bike	Others
₩₩	₩₩	III	II	I
₩₩	₩₩			
II				

WHERE DO YOU LIVE?

Carr	Langley	Ashby	Bonsall	Others (Middleton)
₩₩	₩₩	₩₩	IIII	I
₩₩	I			
II				

3 Either draw a map from memory to show your route to school or describe your route to school.

4 Ask your friends in your class how they travel to school and where they come from. Draw a graph and **flow diagram** like Camla did and explain what they show. Are they similar to Camla's?

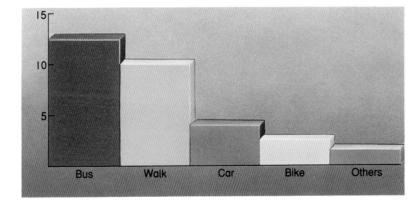

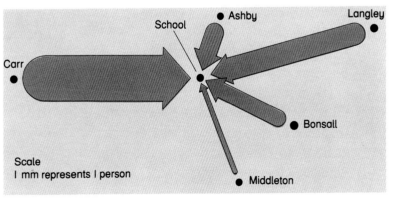

Scale
1 mm represents 1 person

43

Roads and Railways

Links between cities in Britain

Roads and railways are our major means of transport. They link up our major cities.

TRAFFIC NEWS

The M6 is closed between junctions 18 to 20 due to major repair work. Please follow diversion.
Rail strikes hit northern region.
Petrol prices rise again.
Fog causes accident on A1 in Lincolnshire.

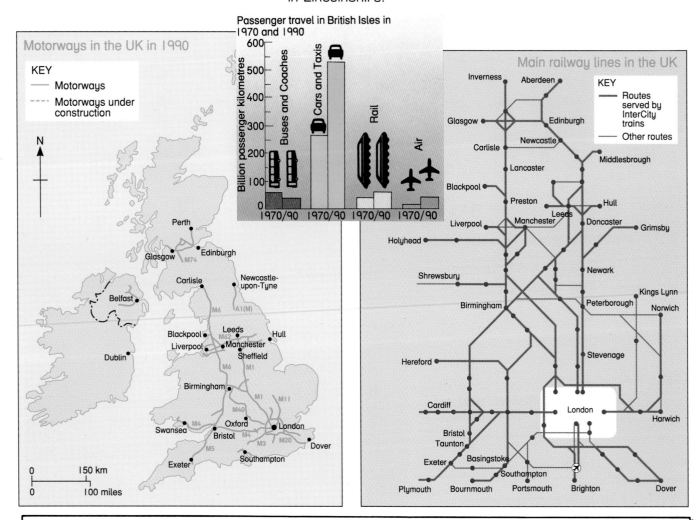

1 Which motorways would you use to travel between:
(a) London and Blackpool
(b) Southampton and Liverpool
(c) Leeds and Bristol
(d) Glasgow and Manchester?
2 Is it possible to travel by rail from:
(a) London to Leeds
(b) Glasgow to Manchester

(c) Bristol to Southampton?
For each journey describe which route you would take.
3 (a) Which was the most common form of passenger transport in 1970?
(b) Which method of transport decreased between 1970 and 1990?
(c) How many billion passenger kilometres of rail were there in 1990?

Links within a city in Japan

TRAFFIC NEWS
The Chuo motorway 13 km from Tokyo is closed due to traffic works. Traffic is very heavy on all routes into Tokyo as rush hour reaches its peak.
Typhoons hit Japan. Transport at a standstill.

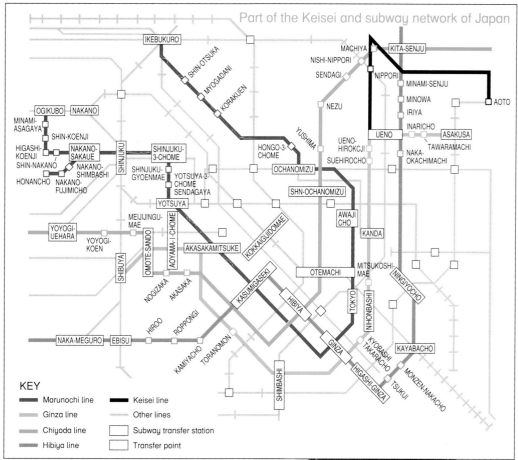

Part of the Keisei and subway network of Japan

KEY
— Marunochi line
— Ginza line
— Chiyoda line
— Hibiya line
— Keisei line
···· Other lines
☐ Subway transfer station
☐ Transfer point

In many places in the world underground railways are used to help ease the problem of traffic **congestion**. People tend to make shorter journeys in cities. Underground railways make travel easier.

Above is a part of a map of the Underground system in Tokyo in Japan. The trains are so busy here that 'pushers' are employed to push as many people as possible onto the trains. This map is called a topological map. It shows no scale or precise direction. It does however show how places link up.

Kannon Temple

Study the map carefully and then answer the following questions.
4 How would you get to and from the following places and which stations would you pass through?
(a) From Tokyo to the Kannon Temple at Akakusa
(b) From the Imperial Palace at Otemachi to Ueno
(c) From home at Ebisu to the Ginza.

5 Work in groups of three or four. You will need an atlas to help you. You are planning a holiday in Japan for yourself and three other friends. You need to decide how to get from your home to your hotel at Otemachi. Plan your route. Include:
(a) methods of travel for each stage of the journey
(b) places visited on the way.
Make a poster to show your route and results.

The Shortest Route

The shortest route between two places is a straight line. However it is not always possible to build roads and railways in a straight line. Many factors have to be considered in building new routes and explaining the course of existing routes. Both natural features and those caused by humans have to be considered.

Which way do routes go?

Reasons why routes do not follow a straight line include:

Different forms of transport in the Derwent Valley at Matlock

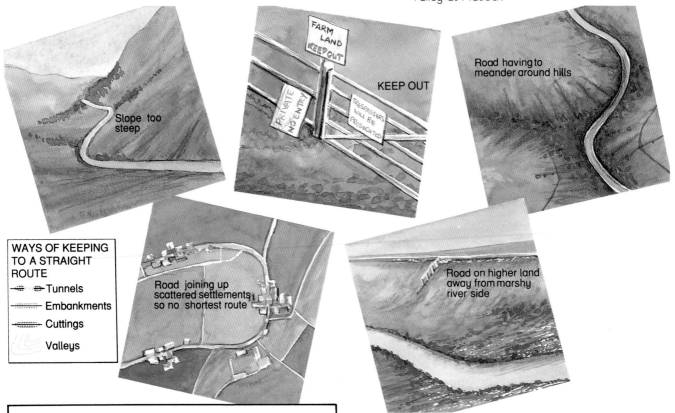

Slope too steep

FARM LAND KEEP OUT
PRIVATE NO ENTRY
TRESPASSERS WILL BE PROSECUTED
KEEP OUT

Road having to meander around hills

WAYS OF KEEPING TO A STRAIGHT ROUTE
- Tunnels
- Embankments
- Cuttings
- Valleys

Road joining up scattered settlements so no shortest route

Road on higher land away from marshy river side

Look at the Ordnance Survey map of the Matlock area in the Peak District in Derbyshire.

1 Find the routes of the A6, River Derwent, and railway line from Matlock station grid reference 296603 to Whatstandwell station grid reference 334542.
2 Make a copy of the following table.
(a) Look at grid square 3353 on the map
(b) What is the land like on the left hand side of the road, railway and river?

(c) Tick the box in the correct column on the table.

Left or Right hand side of road, river and railway	Description of valley sides	Grid square							
		3353		2958		3155		3451	
		L	R	L	R	L	R	L	R
	wooded urban steep sided gentle sides	✓ ✓							

46

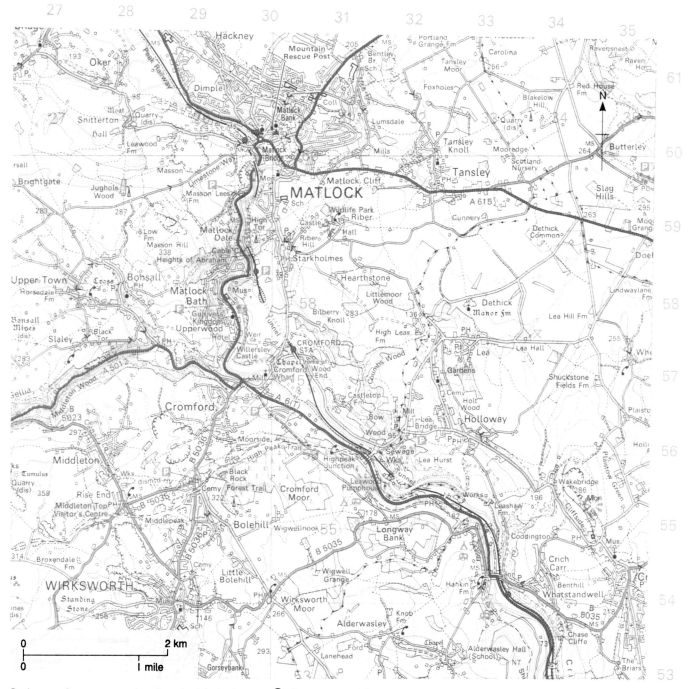

Ordnance Survey map showing the Matlock area © Crown copyright

3 (a) What is the land like on the right hand side of the road, railway and river?

(b) Tick the box in the correct column on the table. The first grid square has been done for you. Do the same for the other three grid squares.

4 (a) From your table say if the road, railway and river all follow the same route. If so why is this?

(b) Is it the shortest route?

5 (a) How far is it in a straight line between Matlock station and Whatstandwell station?

(b) How far is it between these two places following the route of the A6?

6 What has happened to the railway in grid square 3057?

Solving Traffic Problems

Sometimes traffic in our towns becomes so congested that we have to think of ways of easing the amount of traffic. There are many ways including one way systems, **Park and Ride**, bus lanes and building bypasses. Can you think of some others? However, by altering the road systems to help to ease the flow of traffic we can sometimes create other problems.

Building a bypass

When a main road through a town becomes congested it is sometimes possible to build a **bypass**. This is what happened in Chapel-en-le-Frith in Derbyshire.

Traffic congestion

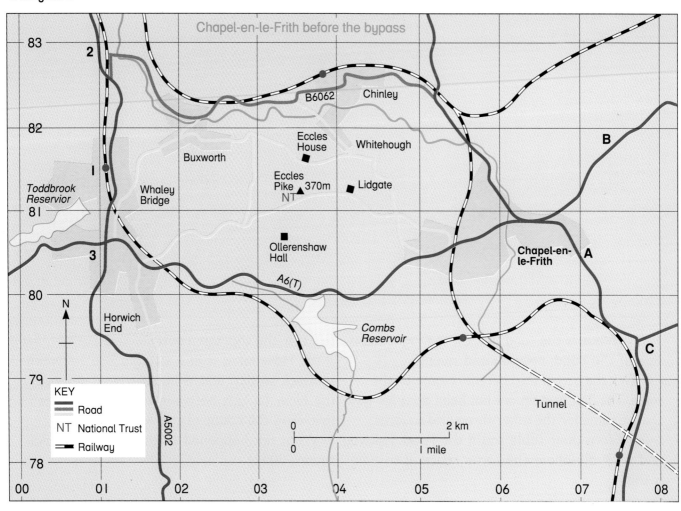

Chapel–en–le–Frith before the bypass

The A6 road ran through Derbyshire to Greater Manchester. It went through the narrow streets of Chapel-en-le-Frith and Whaley Bridge, carrying heavy lorries as well as cars and buses. Roads from Chesterfield and Sheffield linked onto the A6. The A6 was the main shopping street in Chapel-en-le-Frith. The road surfaces were being damaged by the weight of the traffic. The many large lorries carrying crushed stone from the nearby limestone quarries were polluting the area. There had been some accidents. Traffic jams were quite common. Along the sides of the roads there were yellow lines in some places to prevent parking. Cars and other traffic parked where they could. A bypass had to be built – but where?

The survey opposite shows the amount of traffic passing through Chapel-en-le-Frith. Much of this traffic would not be local and so would use a bypass if built. There would be less traffic congestion in the town centre and pedestrians would be able to cross the road more easily.

Length of Survey 20 minutes	
Traffic Survey in Chapel-en-le-Frith before the bypass	
Cars	220
Vans	25
HGV	18
Buses	6
Others	6

1 Look at the map of the area. Where would you build the bypass? Here are some points you must remember when planning the route of your bypass:
- There are three possible starting points A, B or C.
- There are three possible finishing points 1, 2 or 3.
- You must avoid Chapel-en-le-Frith and Whaley Bridge.
- Do not go through National Trust property.
- It should be a direct route as longer routes cost more money.
- It should not cross other main roads and railways if at all possible. Bridges can be built but they are expensive.
- Do not go through settlements and farms if you can help it.

Trace a copy of the map. Draw the route of your bypass on the map.
2 Is the route longer or shorter than the original route?
3 List a group of people who would be in favour of the building of the bypass and say why.
4 List a group of people who would be against the building of the bypass and say why.
5 Write a letter to the Press putting your case either for or against the building of the bypass. You may wish to word-process your letter.

What Did the People Think?

When a bypass is being built in an area there are often lots of different opinions about the different routes and whether or not a bypass should be built. Here are some opinions which the people may have had about the Chapel-en-le-Frith bypass.

Chapel-en-le-Frith before the bypass

FRED JONES Local Resident —
I have just bought my house on the route of the proposed bypass. I would like to see it diverted. It is bound to be much noisier. The building of the by-pass would decrease the value of my house.

KEVIN WILLIAMS Local Councillor —
It may be possible to widen the roads in Chapel-en-le-Frith. The cost of the bypass would be too expensive and this would mean fewer amenities for the area. We ought to look at other possibilities.

GILL ASKEW Local Shop Owner —
I own a shop on the main street. It is very busy and a lot of people stop to buy goods. Parking on the roads is a problem although it is restricted in some areas. Many local people will still come and they will find it easier to shop if there is less traffic.

SABEENA KHAN Local Resident —
I am 70 years old and have lived in Chapel-en-le-Frith for 30 years. I have seen many changes in the area and the amount of traffic is getting larger and larger. The big heavy lorries are the worst. I am looking forward to the building of the bypass. It will be much safer and quieter for me when I do my shopping. There will also be a lot less pollution.

50

CARLA SIJMONS Environmentalist – Another bypass! Why ruin more of the countryside? All this concrete and tarmac. I feel sorry for the wild life. It is bound to ruin many of their natural habitats.

The new bypass

KERRY THOMPSON Long Distance Lorry Driver–
I travel regularly between Buxton and Manchester and it can be a nightmare to go through Chapel-en-le-Frith. I am really looking forward to the building of the bypass. The sooner the better. The roads at present are so narrow. They were not built for such large lorries.

JOHN CROSS Garage Owner –
I own a garage on the A6. At present I get a lot of passing trade. If the by-pass is built I expect my trade will decrease because drivers will have to go out of their way to come to my garage. I know I will still get local trade – but this is not enough.

MARY GREEN Police Officer –
The traffic in Chapel-en-le-Frith can be very bad, especially in the morning and at night when the children go to and from school. I think that if they build the bypass there will be far fewer traffic jams and Chapel-en-le-Frith will be a quieter town.

1 Which four people were in favour of building the bypass?
2 Give two reasons why.
3 Which four people were not in favour of building the bypass?
4 Give two reasons why.
5 Imagine you are a reporter for local radio. You can interview either (a) a person living in the area or (b) a manager of a local firm. Choose one of these people and write down what you think they would say.

6 (a) Join up with three other pupils in your class.
(b) Read all the points of view of the people on these two pages.
(c) Imagine you are a planning group. You have to make a decision whether or not to build a bypass.
(d) Give three reasons for your answer.
(e) Share your ideas with the rest of the class.

u n i t **6**

ALL
CHANGE

North Sea

N

Glasgow   Edinburgh

Newcastle-upon-Tyne

Belfast

Leeds

Dublin   Liverpool   Manchester

Birmingham   Woodford Halse

Cardiff   Bristol

Southampton   London

0   150 km
0   100 miles

All settlements change. Today most settlements are growing. This change and growth has been going on for hundreds of years. When we look at change in a village we see new houses or shops. We need to search for clues as to why the change took place in the past and is taking place today.

How are the people in the village affected by the change? How do the changes affect the type of people in the village? How do the changes affect the jobs of the people in the villages?

Woodford Halse: a changing village

Woodford Halse is in Northamptonshire. It is 15 km north east of Banbury, 20 km west south west of Northampton, 10 km south of Daventry and 15 km north west of Brackley.

At one time there were three villages here, Woodford, Hinton and Farndon. They were mentioned over 1000 years ago in the Domesday Book. Now these villages have joined together to become Woodford Halse.

The village lies in the pretty Northamptonshire countryside in the valley of a small river.

The country is hilly farmland which is used for growing crops. The older houses of the village are made of lovely red brown limestone and are very attractive. The village is very peaceful.

Woodford Halse

Village cottages in Woodford Halse

> I Look at the two photographs of and information on Woodford Halse.
>
> (a) Give two reasons why you might like to live in this village.
>
> (b) Give two reasons why you might NOT wish to live in this village.

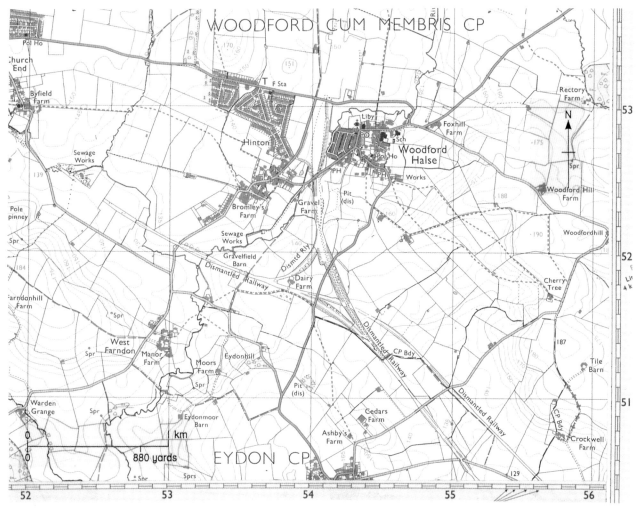

Ordnance Survey map of Woodford Halse
© Crown copyright

2 Complete the diagram below using the information about Woodford Halse.

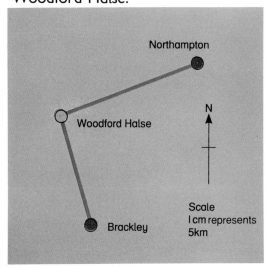

3 Look at the map above.
(a) In which grid square is Woodford Halse?
(b) Make a list of the types of buildings shown on the map which you would find in Woodford Halse.
(c) Which type of buildings would you find in the village which are not shown on the map?
(d) Look at the grid line from 5451 to 5651. Complete the following sentences:
The height of the land at 5451 is _____ m.
From 5451 to 5551, the land slopes up/down.
From 5551 to 5651, the land slopes up/down.
The height of the land at 5651 is _____ m.
(e) Which form of transport is no longer in use at Woodford Halse?
4 Write four sentences about the area in which you live.

The Railway Age

It was over 100 years ago when the railway came to Woodford Halse. In those days the village was no more than a collection of farm workers' cottages.

The village was an important junction of the Great Central Line, passing from London to Sheffield and Manchester.

The crew in front of their locomotive at Woodford Halse in 1906

About 500 men worked on the railways here, as drivers, engineers and labourers. The locomotives had to be looked after, filled with coal, cleaned out and wagons had to be shunted into sidings.

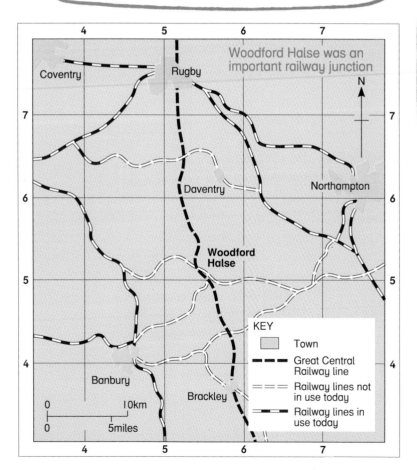

Woodford Halse was an important railway junction

N

Coventry
Rugby
Daventry
Northampton
Woodford Halse
Banbury
Brackley

KEY
Town
Great Central Railway line
Railway lines not in use today
Railway lines in use today

0   10km
0   5miles

Coal from the Nottinghamshire coalfield was sent to Woodford Halse to be put into wagons and taken to many different locations in the south of England.

54 locomotives were based at Woodford Halse, together with wagons. There were many sheds and yards.

Locomotives would return to Woodford Halse every few days to pick up more wagons to take loads up and down England

These were the houses the Great Central Railway built for the workers. I live in one of these. They are small but well built.

Workers houses at Woodford Halse

" When the railway closed many of us went to work on the railways in other main towns. But public transport to other towns was difficult so many of us became unemployed. "

" Today all that is left of the old railway lines are the empty cuttings and embankments through the countryside. "

" But the railways were losing money and in 1966 under British Rail Chairman Dr Beeching the lines were closed. When this happened the railway workers were no longer needed and we lost our jobs. "

" The effect of the closure on the village was dramatic. There was no money around, so other jobs in the village suffered too, for example shopkeeper, publican and coal deliverer. "

1 One hundred years ago the railway was the most important form of transport in the country. Give reasons why it was so important.

2 By 1966 when the railway at Woodford Halse was closed people were using another form of transport; what was this?

3 Look at the map of the railway network at Woodford Halse.

(a) Which towns do railway lines from Woodford Halse go to?

(b) If you had travelled from Banbury to Northampton in 1960 would you have travelled through Woodford Halse?

4 (a) Why was Woodford Halse such an important railway junction?

(b) What were the jobs of the railway workers?

5 Look at the picture of the railway workers' houses.

EITHER

(a) Draw a sketch of the houses and label as many features as you can.

OR

(b) Write a short description of the railway workers' houses at Woodford Halse.

6 The Ordnance Survey map of Woodford Halse shows the tracks of the disused railway lines. Join with a friend and try to decide how these long strips of land could be used today.

The Motorway Age

Woodford Halse is still changing. Some people who are tired of the problems of living in cities have bought houses in and around Woodford Halse. Some of the village people are pleased to welcome the newcomers.

New houses in Woodford Halse

The M40, London to Birmingham, opened in 1991

KEY

=== M40

0 _____ 60 km
0 _____ 40 miles

The M40, London to Birmingham motorway opened January 1991

The M40 was opened in 1991. It means that Woodford Halse has become an attractive place to live for people who work in nearby cities.

1 Why are some people tired of living in London?

2 Give two reasons why they are looking forward to their weekends in Woodford Halse.

3 Look at the road map of part of Great Britain. The completion of the M40 in 1991 makes it easier for people to travel to work in nearby cities from Woodford Halse. To find out which cities they are likely to work in, rank the cities by distance.

4 Why are some villagers in Woodford Halse worried about the arrival of newcomers?

The new M40 – opening ceremony

The Future in Woodford Halse

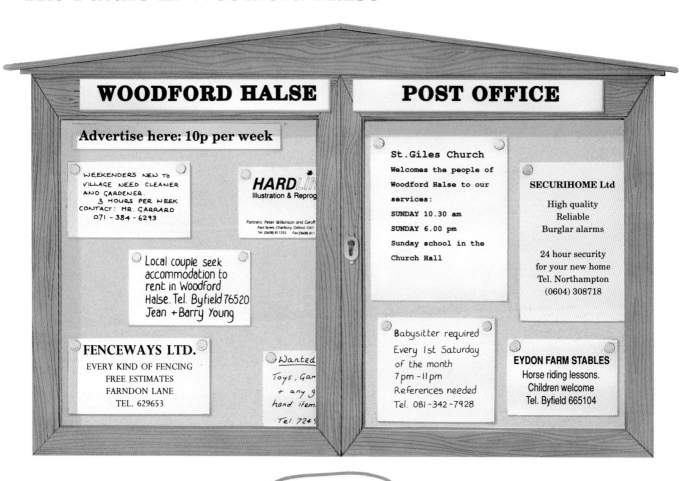

1 Look at the advertisements in Woodford Halse Post Office window.
(a) Name four services which the newcomers to Woodford Halse need.
(b) Why are Jean and Barry Young facing difficulties in finding accommodation in Woodford Halse?

2 Imagine you live in Woodford Halse and are joining in with the discussion on this page.
Write a speech bubble to show what you would say in the discussion.

British Rail has sold a plot of land in Woodford Halse to a local builder. Planning permission has been given for an estate of 12 properties.

Work in groups to plan the layout of houses on the estate.

1 You will need the following equipment:
- an A3 sized sheet of paper to be used as the site of the estate.
- the houses templates (12 outline houses)
- glue, scissors, coloured crayons

2 Remember to follow these rules:
- roads are needed to give access to the houses
- parking is needed for one car per house
- a path is needed to each house
- a park area should be planned
- the estate should be attractive
- it should be easy to use. For example, think about safety from cars and finding your way around

3 Cut out your 12 houses (1) and make them up as shown (2).

2

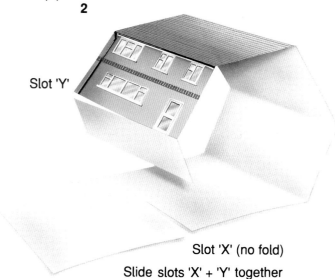

Slot 'Y'

Slot 'X' (no fold)

Slide slots 'X' + 'Y' together

4 Arrange the houses on the estate. When you are satisfied with the layout of houses, glue them firmly into place. Add the extra features to the estate, like roads, paths, parks, etc.

5 When your estate is complete, present it to another group, explaining the good points about the layout.

1

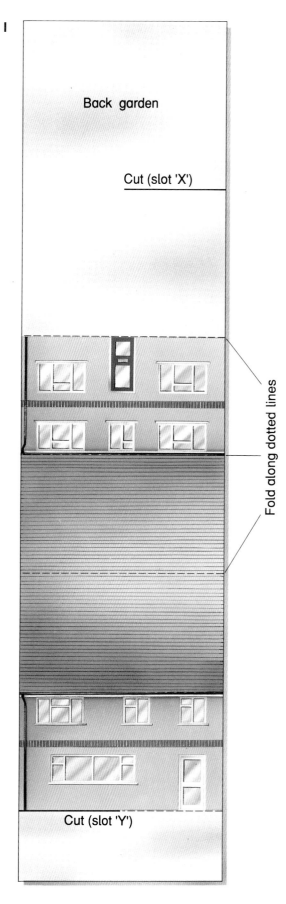

Back garden

Cut (slot 'X')

Fold along dotted lines

Cut (slot 'Y')

unit 7

BATTLE FOR LAND

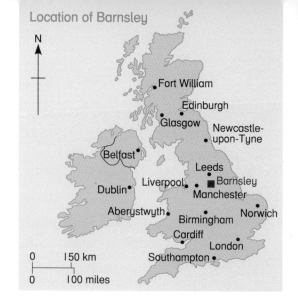
Location of Barnsley

In Britain, the land is used in many different ways. Farming and industry sometimes want to use the same piece of land.

Competition for land between farming and industry

Using the land for farming

Farming is just one important land use in Britain. There are several different types of farming.

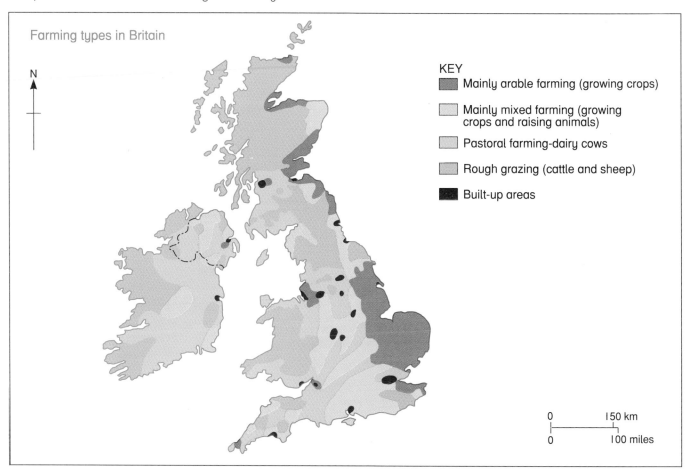
Farming types in Britain

KEY

▨ Mainly arable farming (growing crops)

▢ Mainly mixed farming (growing crops and raising animals)

▢ Pastoral farming-dairy cows

▢ Rough grazing (cattle and sheep)

■ Built-up areas

How we use the land

A

B

C

D

"I wonder why arable farming and rough grazing are carried out in different parts of Britain?"

"Perhaps it's something to do with the land and the **climate**."

1 Look at the key for the farming types in Britain map and the sketches of different farming types.
(a) Match the labels in the key with the correct sketches above.
(b) Write a sentence to show what each of these words mean: arable, pastoral, mixed farming, rough grazing.
2 Look at the map of farming types in Britain.
(a) Draw onto an outline map of Britain areas of rough grazing and arable farming. Give your map a title and a key.

3 Find maps of relief (the shape of the land) and rainfall in the atlas.
(a) Finish these sentences by choosing the correct word from the box below.
Rough grazing is mainly found in the _____ and _____ of Britain. These areas have _____ 1000 mm of rainfall. The relief is mainly _____.
  Arable farming is mainly found in the _____ of Britain. These areas have _____ 1000 mm of rainfall. The relief is mainly _____ .

north, south, east, west, more than, less than, highland, lowland

4 What type of farming would you expect to find near (a) Aberystwyth (b) Norwich (c) Fort William?

Using the Land for Industry

Some of the land in Britain is used for manufacturing industries. These are industries which make products or parts for products. An example of Britain's manufacturing industry is iron and steel.

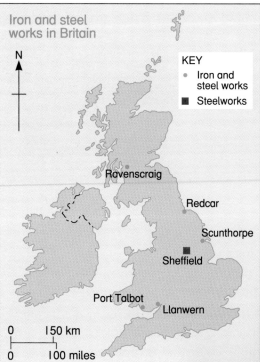

"Are iron and steel works found all over Britain or are there certain patterns in their location?"

"We could look at a map of the location to see if there are any patterns."

margarine	wardrobes
coins	fertiliser
car bodies	knives
teapots	concrete
polyester	garden spade

Products

Iron and steel are made from coal, iron ore and limestone. These are raw materials. In the past, the raw materials came from Britain, but now some are transported to Britain in huge ships from other countries.

Iron and steel works in Britain

N

KEY
• Iron and steel works
■ Steelworks

Ravenscraig
Redcar
Scunthorpe
Sheffield
Port Talbot
Llanwern

0   150 km
0   100 miles

Raw material	Source (where it comes from)
Coal	USA, Canada, Australia, Poland
Iron ore	West Africa, Canada, South America, Australia, Spain
Limestone	Wales, Somerset

Port Talbot Steelworks

62

"Here is the huge iron and steelworks at Port Talbot in South Wales. It was built on a large area of fairly flat coastal land."

A

B

C

D

Look at the box containing the names of products.

1 Make a list of the products which are made in the iron and steel industry.

2 What are the raw materials used to make iron and steel?

3 What form of transport is used to bring the raw materials to Britain?

4 Look at the map of the iron and steelworks.

(a) How many of the iron and steelworks are close to the coast?

(b) Why do you think they are located close to the coast?

5 Look at the photograph of the Port Talbot iron and steelworks.

Here is a list of labels for the photograph

• deep water ore terminal
• iron and steelworks
• labour force living nearby
• good road and rail transport to markets in big towns

Write out these labels and at the side of each one write out the matching letter (A–D) from the photograph.

6 The Sheffield steelworks shown on the map uses scrap steel to make high quality steel products like saws, files and instruments.

(a) Describe the location of the Sheffield steelworks.

(b) Why do you think a coastal location is not important for Sheffield steelworks?

(c) Look at the map of motorway routes in Britain, on page 44. Name an advantage of the location of Sheffield's steel industry.

Farming Land Use in Barnsley

Rob Royd Farm is found near Barnsley in South Yorkshire. The land is too hilly, temperatures are too low and rainfall is too high for arable farming. It is a good location for keeping animals and growing feed crops.

"I'm Jean White and I'm the farmer at Rob Royd. It's a mixed farm. Crops of barley and wheat are grown. Some of the grain is fed to the beef cattle which are kept in barns all year round. We also keep hens – in controlled conditions in the hen houses."

Feed store

Yard

Barn

Cattle sheds

Farm house

Hen houses

KEY

☐ Fields belonging to Rob Royd Farm

0   km   1

Ordnance Survey map showing the land of Rob Royd Farm © Crown copyright

"My farm is **85 hectares**. The land is fairly hilly in places, and this affects the machinery I can use. Before World War II, the land was used for surface mining. I often come across the waste from the mining when I'm ploughing. The soil is quite clayey in parts. Although it is hard to plough it does hold the water during dry summers. It's quite cool and damp here during **most of the year.**"

Farm Machinery

Baler

Combine

Seed drill

Hen houses

Irrigator

Grading eggs

Tractor

Jean White keeps 9000 hens and they lay about 50 000 eggs every week. She makes 90 deliveries a week to local shops, restaurants, milk deliverers, bakers and canteens.

Enquiry: What sort of farming at Rob Royd?

We can show the farming at Rob Royd as a systems diagram:

INPUTS	PROCESSES	OUTPUTS
_____	growing cereal crops	cereal crops – barley – wheat
shape and height of the land (relief)		
_____		
machinery weather	raising beef cattle	beef cattle

1 Use the information about Rob Royd Farm to finish off the systems diagram opposite. Choose the correct words from the box:

eggs	raising hens
buildings	soil

2 Draw a picture of one of the inputs. Write a sentence about it.
3 Use all the inputs to explain why Rob Royd land is used for farming.

Industrial Land use in Barnsley

Barnsley is changing. Closing down the coalmines has brought high unemployment. Barnsley Council plans to bring industry back into the area. It plans to build industrial estates. These are areas planned for factories, warehouses and other industrial uses. Some of the industrial estates will be on land which has been left **derelict** following the closure of mines. Others will be built on land that is supposed to be kept as countryside (Green Belt land).

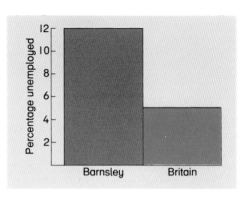

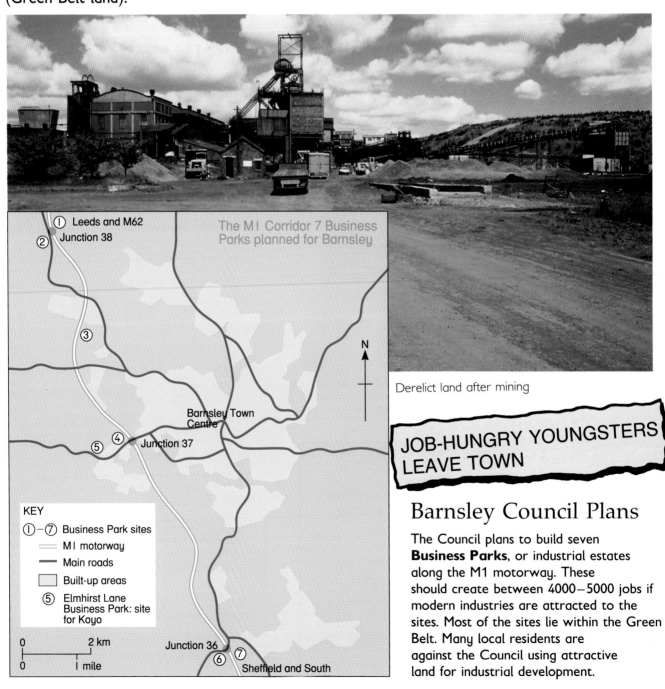

Derelict land after mining

JOB-HUNGRY YOUNGSTERS LEAVE TOWN

Barnsley Council Plans

The Council plans to build seven **Business Parks**, or industrial estates along the M1 motorway. These should create between 4000–5000 jobs if modern industries are attracted to the sites. Most of the sites lie within the Green Belt. Many local residents are against the Council using attractive land for industrial development.

KEY
- ①–⑦ Business Park sites
- M1 motorway
- Main roads
- Built-up areas
- ⑤ Elmhirst Lane Business Park: site for Koyo

0   2 km
0   1 mile

Koyo comes to Barnsley!

Elmhirst Lane Business Park is close to Junction 37 of the M1 motorway. The Business Park is being developed on an old colliery site. A Japanese firm, Koyo Bearings (Europe) Ltd is building a manufacturing plant at the Business Park. Koyo Bearings makes parts for cars. The new factory will produce 24 million sets of bearings a year. Most of these will be exported to other European countries.

Elmhirst Lane Business Park, Barnsley

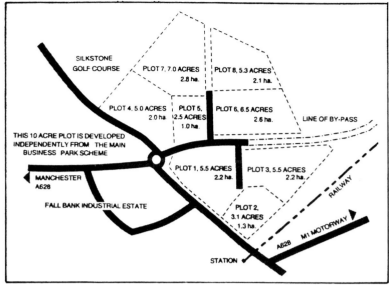

Elmhirst Lane Business Park

"We chose this site for several reasons. There is a skilled labour force and experienced managers nearby. There are very good transport links. The Government and Barnsley Council have helped the company to set up the factory here."

1 Give two of Barnsley's problems.
2 How does Barnsley Council plan to solve these problems?
3 Imagine you are a reporter working for the Barnsley Chronicle. Barnsley Council has just completed the deal with Koyo Bearings to build a factory at the Elmhirst Lane Business Park near Barnsley. (Site number 5 on the map.)
Prepare a story for your local readers, giving the reasons why Koyo Bearings chose Barnsley for its new factory. You could use desk top publishing computer software to present your report.

Business Parks or Green Belt for Barnsley?

Barnsley Council plans to use the land next to Junction 37 of the M1 motorway as a new Business Park. The land is used for farming at the moment, and is part of Barnsley Green Belt. The Council has arranged a public meeting at Dodworth village library to present the plans and to listen to the views of local people.

JUNCTION 37 – LAND USE CHANGES

Jean White, farmer
"The Council plans to build the Business Park on part of my land. The M1 corridor contains the best Green Belt land in Barnsley. The green and leafy landscape is a delight to drivers who pass by. If the Council's plans go ahead, I'll lose 10% of my livelihood. In my view, the Council has grossly exaggerated the number of jobs that will be created. The warehousing and haulage firms which move onto these sites don't need a large labour force ... "

Joseph Field, Dodworth village resident and leader of Residents Against Green Belt Exploitation (RAGE)
"Our main argument against the plan is: Why take attractive countryside for industrial use when there are derelict colliery sites and higher unemployment to the east of Barnsley?
  The community spirit of Dodworth will be destroyed if this plan goes ahead: the village will be *yuppified* by outsiders and local people will be left with a few poorly paid jobs which nobody else wants ... "

Katherine Chang, Dodworth resident and conservation worker
"I'm concerned about the spread of the built-up area into the countryside. Footpath walks will be spoilt; increased traffic, especially heavy lorries will produce noise, pollution, vibration and the danger of accidents. Wild life around the village will be devastated ... "

Boundary of Business Park

Removal of Green Belt

Revised Green Belt

Housing Site

Site for Allotments

Arjun Vedi, Planning Officer, Barnsley Council
"The Green Belt boundaries were drawn up when industry in Barnsley was underground: now it's time to take a second look because of changing industries. There has been an increase in Green Belt area in the last 8 years. These plans involve a tiny loss of Green Belt. We have received many enquiries from firms interested in the site: accessibility from the motorway is a key factor. Derelict colliery sites to the east of Barnsley do not have this accessibility . . . "

Jane Williams, Leader of Barnsley Council
"Unemployment in Barnsley is high. These Business Parks will create 4000–5000 jobs for the Barnsley area. We have such a lot to offer; an adaptable, experienced workforce, accessibility to the M1, government and council assistance for new companies. We would be foolish not to take up the challenge. Without this plan, the future looks bleak for Barnsley: young people are moving away and standards of living are declining . . . "

John Sykes, ex-coalminer at Dodworth colliery
"I was made redundant in 1985 when the pit closed. I support the Council's plans to develop the Business Park. I welcome the prospect of new jobs coming into the area. Barnsley needs a new image. New people moving in, plus jobs for local people will bring prosperity: shops, leisure facilities, transport links and homes will all be improved as the area develops. We must move with the times . . . "

The Public Meeting, Dodworth Village Library

1 Which people are in favour of the Junction 37 Business Park being built?
2 Give three reasons why they are in favour.
3 Which people are against the Business Park being built?
4 Give three reasons why they are against the plan.
5 Do you think that the Business Parks should be built on Green Belt land? Give your reasons.

TREATING
WATER WELL

u n i t 8

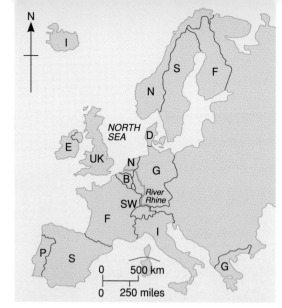

C lean water is an essential resource. In European countries there are times of water shortages. The levels of **pollution** in many rivers, lakes and seas are increasing. How can the problems of an unreliable and polluted water environment be overcome?

Reservoir in Wales – notice the low level of the water

Uses of Water
In homes   In farming

In industry

Coates Ale Brewery

WATER SHORTAGE: HOSEPIPE BANS ACROSS BRITAIN

Low rainfall and high evaporation rates mean that water restrictions are firmly in place in many parts of Britain. Parts of East Anglia, Kent, Yorkshire and Lincolnshire are experiencing the worst drought for 25 years.

Rivers in the east of Britain are flowing at very low levels and **ground water** is more than 40% lower than normal.

Demand for increased supplies of water continue to rise by 1–2% per year.

The water mains, installed by Victorians, need replacing. In south west Britain, a third of all water supplies is lost due to leakage from mains.

15th August, 1990

Where does the water in Britain come from?

I RESERVOIRS
River and dam

2 RIVERS
Pumping station and treatment plant
for extracting water

3 AQUIFERS (underground water)

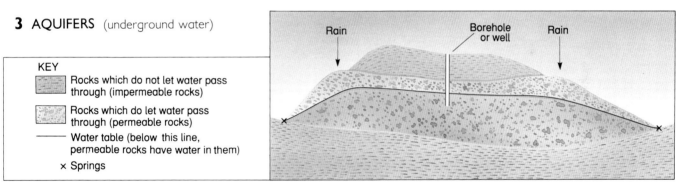

KEY

Rocks which do not let water pass
through (impermeable rocks)

Rocks which do let water pass
through (permeable rocks)

Water table (below this line,
permeable rocks have water in them)

× Springs

Rain   Borehole
or well   Rain

I Why was there a hosepipe ban across
Britain in August 1990?

2 Read all the information on these pages
and finish off this flow diagram, using the
words in the list to help you:

3 Look at the maps of rainfall and population
distribution in Britain in Unit 1 (page 10) or
in an atlas. Suggest a problem these
distributions may cause.

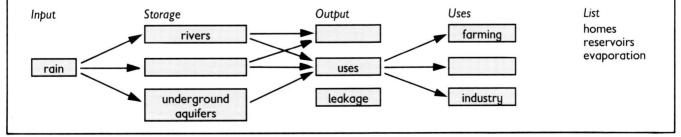

Input	Storage	Output	Uses	List
rain	rivers		farming	homes
		uses		reservoirs
	underground aquifers	leakage	industry	evaporation

71

The Problems of Water Supplies

A Plan for water supplies

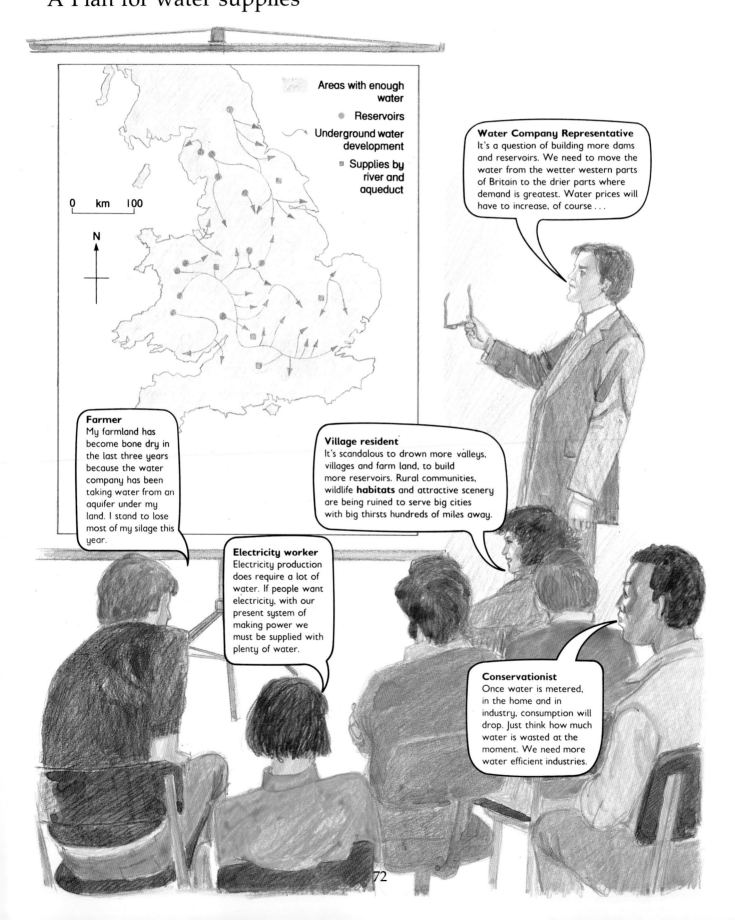

Areas with enough water

Reservoirs

Underground water development

Supplies by river and aqueduct

0 km 100

N

Water Company Representative
It's a question of building more dams and reservoirs. We need to move the water from the wetter western parts of Britain to the drier parts where demand is greatest. Water prices will have to increase, of course . . .

Farmer
My farmland has become bone dry in the last three years because the water company has been taking water from an aquifer under my land. I stand to lose most of my silage this year.

Village resident
It's scandalous to drown more valleys, villages and farm land, to build more reservoirs. Rural communities, wildlife **habitats** and attractive scenery are being ruined to serve big cities with big thirsts hundreds of miles away.

Electricity worker
Electricity production does require a lot of water. If people want electricity, with our present system of making power we must be supplied with plenty of water.

Conservationist
Once water is metered, in the home and in industry, consumption will drop. Just think how much water is wasted at the moment. We need more water efficient industries.

Planning for water in Sweden

It is difficult to believe that in a country with over 100 000 natural lakes, there could be a problem of water supply. Most of the Swedish population live in the south of the country. They need water for their homes, factories and for leisure.

In the 1960s, the water planners in Sweden realised that there would be problems of water supply and water pollution before the year 2000 unless action was taken.

> **THE GOVERNMENT OF SWEDEN: ACTION PLAN FOR WATER**
> By the year 2000, the government plans to reduce water consumption by:
>
> **1** Making the Swedish people aware of the problems of water supply.
> **2** Introducing **water meters** into homes and industries.
> **3** Introducing more water-efficient processes into industries, for example, water recycling.

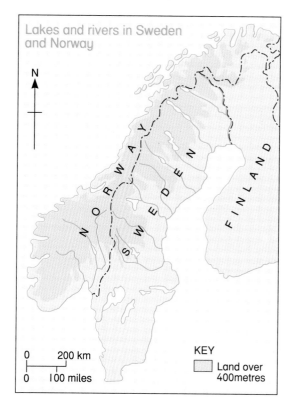

Lakes and rivers in Sweden and Norway

KEY — Land over 400metres

SWEDEN – WATER CONSUMPTION
(How much water is used in Sweden)

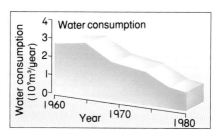

A domestic water meter dial

Read the views of the five people on the opposite page.

1 Imagine you are present at the meeting.
Write a speech bubble giving your own views or agreeing/disagreeing with someone at the meeting.
2 (a) Why has the Swedish government introduced an action plan for water?
(b) Look at the evidence on this page. Have the actions of the government in Sweden brought down the amount of water used in the country?
3 Use the information about water planning in Sweden to decide if Britain should follow the same plan. What are the good points about the plan?

An industrial water meter

Water Pollution . . . . . and solutions

Cities

A lot of people living in a city produce a lot of waste. Chemicals, sewage, household and industrial rubbish may find their way to the river. At least 20% of sewage works are not cleaning sewage to an acceptable standard.

Landfill sites are used to dump household and industrial rubbish. **Decomposition** of the rubbish can produce dangerous gases. Water seeping through rubbish carries dangerous chemicals into rivers.

Acid rain

Factories, power stations and vehicles produce gases which mix with rainwater. This acid rain is dangerous to fish and other water life in rivers and lakes.

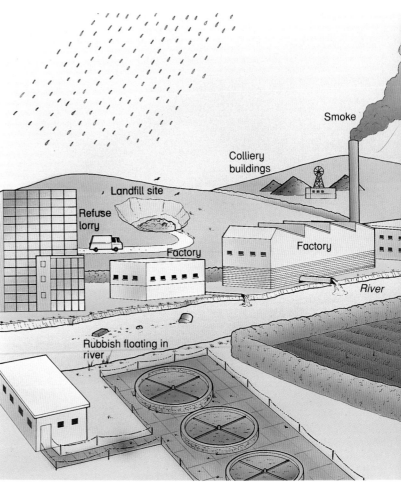

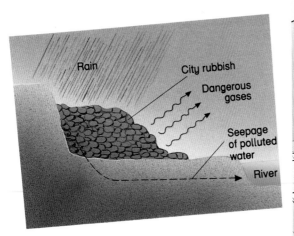

Landfill site

I **How can the problems of water pollution be solved?**

Here is a list of solutions. Sort them out and write them into a copy of the table. Some solutions will work for more than one problem.

Solutions

- use non-polluting, renewable methods to make power, for example the wind.
- make industries pay high taxes for pollution.
- fit catalytic convertors on cars.
- build more efficient sewage works.
- recycle wastes like paper, glass.
- give grants to farmers to farm without chemicals.
- give people compost bins to encourage them to recycle household vegetable waste.
- make industry fit cleaning equipment to its factories.
- teach everyone about the damage that is being done to water.

Industries

Factories, for example, chemical, iron and steel and carpet works release toxic chemicals into river water.

Water seeping through mined land transports harmful materials into rivers.

Power stations

Power stations use water for cooling. The water is returned to the river up to 12° C warmer than when it was removed. This decreases the amount of oxygen dissolved in the water. Many fish and other aquatic animals suffocate with low oxygen levels.

Nuclear power stations cause the release of **radioactive wastes** into water. Although the wastes are low level, they may accumulate in river animals.

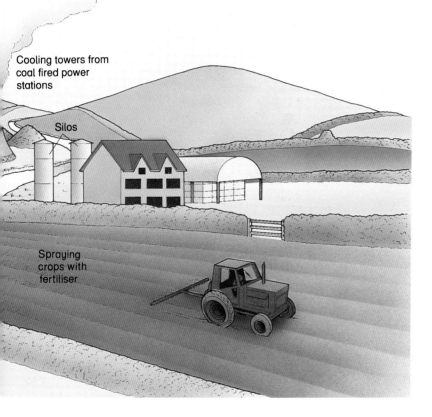

Cooling towers from coal fired power stations

Silos

Spraying crops with fertiliser

Farms

Nitrates from **farmyard** slurry and **fertiliser** pollute rivers. Nitrate levels in ground water and rivers today are very high. Nitrates find their way into drinking water; no one knows the long term effect on people's health.

High nitrate levels in lakes, together with sunshine, make blooms of **blue-green algae** grow. This algae gives out poisons. River creatures and plants die; dogs and farm animals are poisoned; shellfish have been contaminated and people have become seriously ill after using lakes for water sports.

PROBLEM	SOLUTIONS
Cities	
Acid Rain	
Industries	
Power Stations	
Farms	

Who is to blame for the state of the River Rhine?

The water of the River Rhine is pure when it rises in the Swiss Alps. The river flows north, through France, Germany and the Netherlands. It enters the North Sea 1 320 km from its **source**. The water of the River Rhine is not pure when it reaches the North Sea. It has received wastes from agriculture, industry and mines.

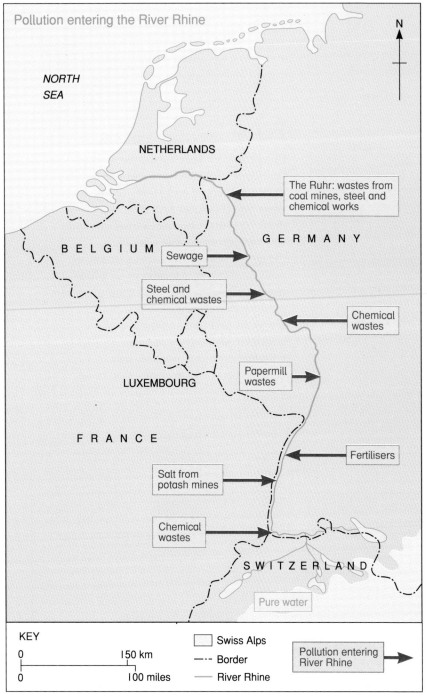

Pollution entering the River Rhine

NORTH SEA

NETHERLANDS

BELGIUM

GERMANY

LUXEMBOURG

FRANCE

SWITZERLAND

The Ruhr: wastes from coal mines, steel and chemical works

Sewage

Steel and chemical wastes

Chemical wastes

Papermill wastes

Fertilisers

Salt from potash mines

Chemical wastes

Pure water

KEY

0   150 km
0   100 miles

☐ Swiss Alps
–··– Border
— River Rhine

➜ Pollution entering River Rhine

Dead fish – the result of accidental chemical release by Sandoz, Switzerland 1969

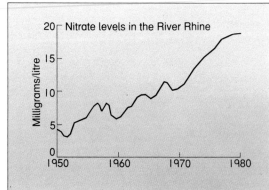

Nitrate levels in the River Rhine

In 1988 about 316 000 tonnes of industrial and agricultural wastes entered the River Rhine.

Annual load of toxins measured where the River Rhine flows into the Netherlands (tonnes)

Lead	1200
Phenols	400
Arsenic	322
Cadmium	80
Poly-chlorinated bi-phenols (used in making pesticides)	20
Mercury	16

1991 River Rhine Pollution Convention

NETHERLANDS

We depend on the waters of the Rhine for a lot of our drinking water, as well as for water for our farmland. We receive polluted water from Switzerland, France and Germany. We feel that this is unfair. Our government is having to pay for expensive water treatment to clean our drinking water.

GERMANY

Most of Germany's industry is located along the River Rhine. The livelihoods of millions of people depend on it. Industries have located there for transport, cooling water and to dump their waste. Our government is developing a plan to introduce a pollution tax on all Rhine industries which use the river for dumping wastes.

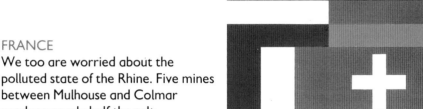

FRANCE

We too are worried about the polluted state of the Rhine. Five mines between Mulhouse and Colmar produce nearly half the salt pollution of the whole river. We hope to develop underground storage for the salt, however underground water may become even more polluted. We would like to suggest that closer monitoring of dumping is carried out, and that industries which dump waste are fined heavily.

SWITZERLAND

Although we do not use the River Rhine as a major source of water, we do own up to polluting it. The 1986 fire at Sandoz chemical factory, near Basle released 30 different agricultural chemicals into the Rhine. 500 000 fish were killed outright, many more were poisoned. We think that the countries of the Rhine should together produce an emergency action plan. It should be used immediately after an incident of accidental pollution.

Industry along the River Rhine at Leverkusen

Work in a group of two or three.
Your aim is to produce a report which:

1 describes the way the River Rhine is being polluted;
2 gives solutions to the problem of river pollution on the Rhine (the previous work on water pollution may be helpful);
3 decides how costs of cleaning up the river should be shared between the four countries. (Rank the countries with the first taking the largest share);
4 describes action to be taken in the future to keep the River Rhine clean.

You could use a word processor to present your report.

Europe's Dustbin

The River Rhine is only one of many rivers which carry pollution into the North Sea dustbin. The North Sea receives the waste of surrounding countries in other ways too...

River pollution

Other rivers, as well as the River Rhine, carry dangerous chemicals from industries and farms into the North Sea. Here are three examples:

River	Mercury tonnes/yr	Cadmium tonnes/yr	Nitrogen thousand tonnes/yr	Phosphorus thousand tonnes/yr
Humber	0.7	3.5	41	0.6
Scheldt	1.0	7.4	62	7.0
Elbe	7.3	8.4	150	12.0

Sewage Sludge

Sewage sludge is produced during the treatment of dirty water at the sewage works. The UK dumps 5 million tonnes of sewage sludge in the sea every year. It may harm marine life.

Unclean beaches

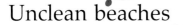

EC finds many British beaches unclean

Many British holiday resorts dump raw sewage into the sea. In 1989, only 22 beaches in Britain were awarded the EC Blue Flag. This award means that the beach and seawater have reached a high standard of cleanliness. Beaches like Cleethorpes, Southend, Great Yarmouth and Scarborough were not awarded a Blue Flag.

THE NORTH
CLEANING

Sewage outfall pipe

Ocean burning

Dangerous chemicals like pesticides are burnt on board ships in the North Sea. The air and sea water are meant to 'dilute' the fumes from the burning process. There is a danger of spilling the chemicals in an accident at sea.

The ocean incinerator ship Vulcanus II burning hazardous waste

Oil pollution

Oil is transported in the North Sea in large tankers. Spills from tankers and washing out of tanks produce oil pollution. Accidents may occur on oil rigs in the North Sea, causing oil pollution of the water.

| 0 | 100 km |
| 0 | 100 miles |

SEA NEEDS
JP

The environmental group, Greenpeace, has suggested ways of cleaning up the North Sea

River pollution:	– trace pollutants to their source and fine polluters
Ocean burning:	– cut down on the amount of waste produced and recycle more waste
Sewage sludge:	– use sludge as a fertiliser, fuel or building material instead of dumping it at sea
Unclean beaches:	– improve the treatment of sewage on the land and make people pay fines for dirtying beaches
Oil spills:	– ban the washing out of tanks at sea and improve the safety of oil tankers and oil rigs

1 Which countries border the North Sea? (An atlas will help.)

2 Cleaning up the North Sea will be a big job. Here are six steps towards organising the clean-up operation, but they are in the wrong order. Sort them out into the right order:
● decide on the action needed in the next five years
● organise a meeting of all North Sea countries
● meet up in five years' time to see if action has been successful
● talk about problems
● decide who will pay for the cleaning up
● develop a plan of action to clean up the North Sea

3 Who do you think should pay for the cleaning up of the North Sea:
● the governments
● industries
● seaside resorts
● t he European Community?
Give reasons for your choice.

u n i t 9 THE EARTH MOVED!

Here we look at how the earth moves. We see how these movements affect people. We see how people try to respond to the hazards caused by earth movements.

Earthquakes and volcanoes are only found on certain parts of the earth. They are mainly found on the edges or margins of the world's plates. A thin shell of the earth's crust is divided into a number of pieces, called plates, which move very slowly across the surface of the earth.

Volcanic eruption

Fertile soil on the side of volcano

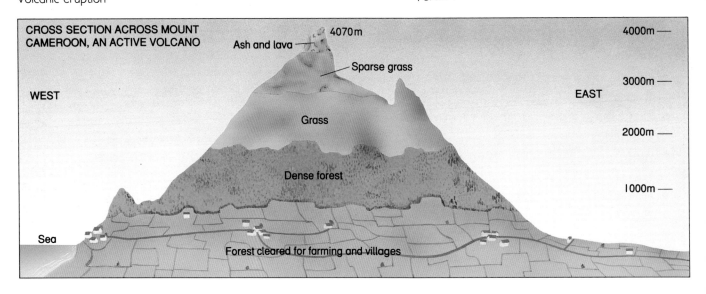

CROSS SECTION ACROSS MOUNT CAMEROON, AN ACTIVE VOLCANO

4070m

Ash and lava

Sparse grass

WEST

Grass

Dense forest

EAST

Sea

Forest cleared for farming and villages

4000m —

3000m —

2000m —

1000m —

80

My name is Rose. I am an official guide taking people to the top of Mount Cameroon, an active volcano. It last erupted in 1982 and before that in 1977. Mostly, it is tourists who wish to be guided to the top.

My name is Moses. I live in Buea on the lower slopes of Mount Cameroon. This is a beautiful area with fertile agricultural land. I remember the last eruption. At first the earth rumbled. Then rock and ash blew into the air forming heavy clouds in the day but bright clouds at night.

Any tourist who does go up must carry their bed on their back. It is a 2 day trip to the top.

Very few tourists take advantage of our services.

The prison is halfway up the mountain. The climate is difficult for the inmates.

We can grow carrots on the mountain. It is cool there.

1 Describe how the vegetation changes as you go up Mount Cameroon. Suggest one reason why these changes occur.
2 Try and explain why people are willing to live near to active or 'live' volcanoes.
3 Read the electronic mail messages sent by Rose to her manager in the Cameroon Tourist Agency in Yaoundé. Prepare a response to send back. It must give advice on how to make a tourist brochure.

MT. CAMEROON 4070 M.
IT IS STRICTLY FORBIDDEN TO CLIMB THE MOUNTAIN WITHOUT AN AUTHORIZATION FROM THE TOURISM OFFICE BUEA. PMB 20, TEL. 32.25.34 ANY INFRINGER CAUGHT WILL PAY A FINE OF 20,000 F.CFA OR ONE MONTH IMPRISONMENT ALL CLIMBERS MUST BE ACCOMPANIED BY OFFICIAL GUIDES PROVIDED BY THE TOURISM OFFICE

Mount Cameroon warning notice

How Hazards are Caused

ALL QUIET   **FIRST RUMBLE**

← ─── First (primary) waves ───   ─── Approximately 5 seconds ───

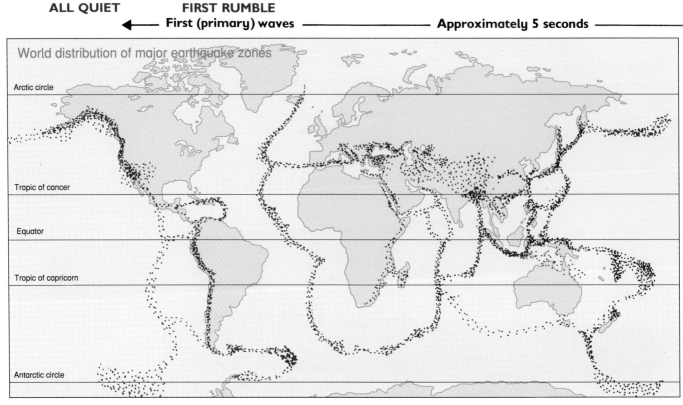

World distribution of major earthquake zones

Arctic circle

Tropic of cancer

Equator

Tropic of capricorn

Antarctic circle

MAJOR EARTHQUAKES OVER A PERIOD OF 30 YEARS

Date	Epicentre	Richter scale	Date	Epicentre	Richter scale	Date	Epicentre	Richter scale
1934 Jan	Bihar, India	8.4	1946 Aug	West Indies	8.1	1957 Mar	Andreanof Is	8.0
July	Santa Cruz Is.	8.1	Dec	Shikoku, Japan	8.4	April	To the south of Samoa	8.0
1935 May	Quetta, Pakistan	7.5	1949 Aug	South Alaska	8.1	July	Guerrero, Mexico	7.5
Dec	Sumatra	8.1	1950 Feb	Hokkaido, Japan	7.9	1958 July	SE Alaska	8.0
1938 Feb	Java	8.6	Aug	Assam	8.7	1959 Jan	Brittany	5.2
1939 Dec	Anatolia	7.9	Dec	New Hebrides	8.1	1960 Feb	North Algeria	5.5
1941 June	Burma	8.7	Dec	Andes, Argentina	8.3	Feb	Agadir, Morocco	5.8
June	Central Australia	6.8	1952 July	Kern County, California	7.7	April	Lar, Iran	5.8
Nov	West Portugal	8.4	1953 Mar	NW Anatolia	7.2	1961 June	Ethiopia	6.8
1942 May	Ecuador	8.3	1954 Sept	El Asnam; Algeria		Aug	Peru/Brazil	7.5
Aug	Guatemala	8.3		(Orleansville)	6.8	1962 Sept	Buyin, Iran	7.5
Aug	Brazil	8.6	1955 Feb	Quetta, Pakistan	6.8	1963 July	Skopje, Yugoslavia	6.0
Nov	To the south of Africa	8.34	1956 Dec	Baja California	6.8	1964 Mar	Anchorage, Alaska	7.5
1943 April	Andes	8.3						
1944 Dec	Honshu, Japan	8.3						

Two readings on a seismograph, or earthquake recording machine. The earthquake at Mt St Helen's lasted 27 minutes. The earth shook because of the hot liquid magma moving through underground cracks

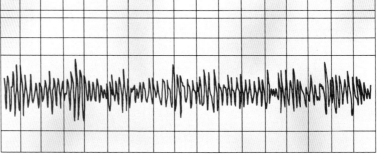

A Earthquake at Mt St Helen's

Second (secondary) waves ——————————————————— **Long waves** ——————

ALL QUIET

The aftermath of an earthquake, San Francisco 1989

Earthquakes take place when the plates move together. These plates make up the crust, the thin outer skin of the earth. They can move apart, collide or scrape together.

There are many ways of trying to predict an earthquake. None of the ways are foolproof. The first evidence of a quake may not be seen until there is a reading on the machine called the **seismograph**.

Once an earthquake happens, a huge clear-up operation begins.

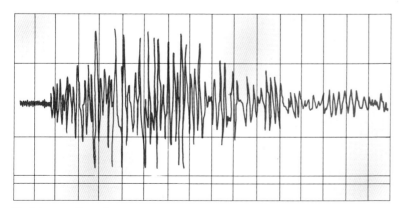

B A 'normal' quake

1 Imagine you are in charge of the clean-up operation after the earthquake. Here is a list of things to do after an earthquake. Put them in order of importance explaining your order.

Turn off power source; disconnect water; get out of all buildings; check for gas; make a count of people who were in the buildings; check on animals and pets; ring the police; hide under furniture in case of after-shocks; go to a park or open space.

2 Look at the seismographs on these pages. They are records of the earthquake's 'waves' or 'shocks'. The bigger the wave or shock, the bigger the 'blip' on the seismograph.

Describe the differences between the earthquakes recorded on seismograph A and seismograph B.

Predicting the Hazard

The effects of a **hazard**, such as an earthquake or volcanic eruption are most severe if it comes as a surprise. Here are some ways in which earthquake activity can be predicted.

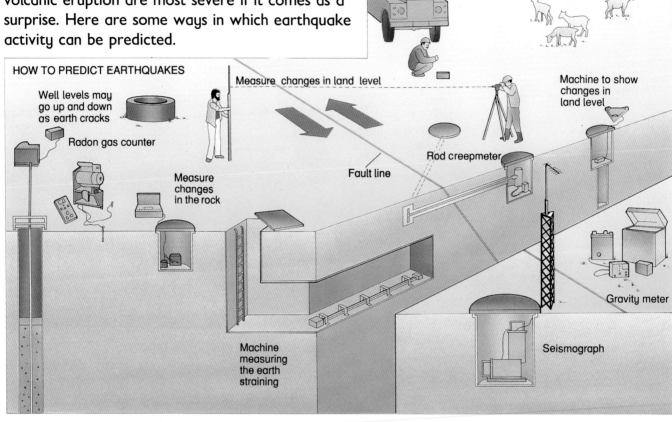

HOW TO PREDICT EARTHQUAKES

Well levels may go up and down as earth cracks

Radon gas counter

Measure changes in land level

Measure changes in the rock

Fault line

Rod creepmeter

Animals become scared

Machine to show changes in land level

Gravity meter

Seismograph

Machine measuring the earth straining

Once the earthquake occurs, it can be measured using a scale, such as the modified Mercalli scale or the Richter scale used in the table below.

1. Detected only by instruments.

2. Slight – felt by people at rest.

3. Moderate – felt by people who are moving about.

4. Strong–slight damage to buildings.

5. Destructive–chimneys fall.

6. Disastrous – many buildings destroyed.

7. Very disastrous – few buildings left standing, ground cracks.

8. Catastrophic – total destruction of buildings, ground badly twisted.

The headlines describe the difficulties
facing people after an earthquake

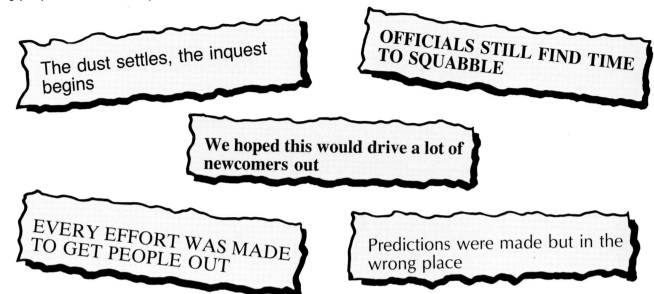

The dust settles, the inquest begins

OFFICIALS STILL FIND TIME TO SQUABBLE

We hoped this would drive a lot of newcomers out

EVERY EFFORT WAS MADE TO GET PEOPLE OUT

Predictions were made but in the wrong place

Source: *The Independent* 20/10/89.

What would you do?

Read the newspaper headlines of 20/10/89 after the San Francisco earthquake. A public meeting is called to discuss the ways in which reconstruction can begin. Five people speak at the meeting; a councillor and the mayor (from the front), and a journalist, a resident who is now homeless and a civil engineer (from the audience).

1 Prepare a speech for one of the people above.
2 Work in groups to share the opinions of others.
3 How will decisions be made?
4 What are the problems in coming to a group decision?

Volcanic Eruptions – Countdown!

We are looking at the reasons for a volcanic eruption. We are also looking at the effects it has on the environment. The example used is Mount St Helen's, which erupted in May 1980.

St Helen's countdown 1980

March 20th   The start of the show. Mount St Helen's wakes up this Thursday with an earthquake of 4.1 on the Richter scale, a scale used to measure earthquakes.

March 25th   Visitors are urged to stay away from the mountain in case an earth tremor or shock causes an avalanche.

March 27th   First ash! There is an explosion at 12.36 pm! A 250 ft crater or hole opens on the summit.

March 29th   Two craters are spotted, which then join up.

April 1st   Ash clouds rise to 20 000 ft above sea level.

April 3rd   Earth tremors noted. Magma, or underground hot lava, is believed to be moving inside the mountain.

April 30th–May 12th   The north side of the mountain bulges visibly.

May 18th   Eruption at 8.32 am. Ash and heat are thrown out in a 156 sq mile area. **Mud flows** dam rivers. Eruption or explosion caused by an earthquake.

May 25th   A less severe eruption strikes a nearby population.

June 12th   More ash thrown out.

June 25th   Seventeen people are now missing, presumed dead.

July 8th   Eleven people are charged with trespassing in the danger zone around the mountain. They are found guilty.

Stages in eruption of Mt St Helen's

Hot lava, Hawaii

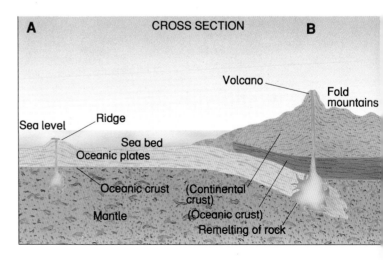

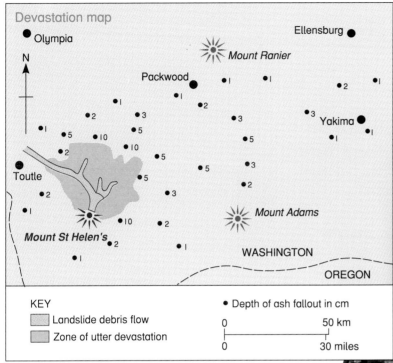

Devastation map

Olympia

Ellensburg

Mount Ranier

Packwood

Yakima

Toutle

Mount St Helen's

Mount Adams

WASHINGTON

OREGON

KEY

Landslide debris flow

Zone of utter devastation

● Depth of ash fallout in cm

0   50 km

0   30 miles

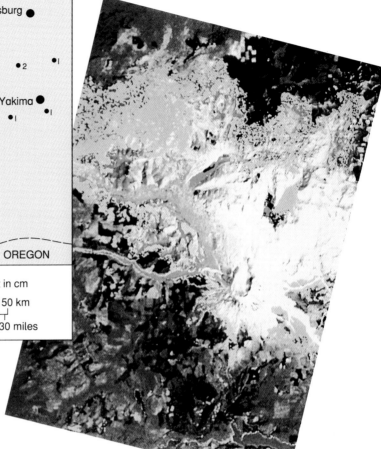

LANDSAT image of area following an eruption

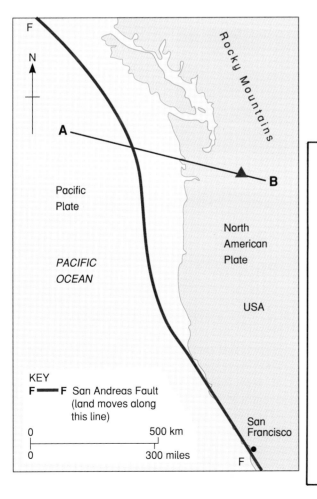

Rocky Mountains

A

B

Pacific Plate

PACIFIC OCEAN

North American Plate

USA

San Francisco

KEY

F━━F San Andreas Fault (land moves along this line)

0   500 km

0   300 miles

1 Using the countdown, explain how and why the eruption occurred. What were the likely effects afterwards?

2 Look at the devastation map. What do you notice about the patterns of ash fall-out?

3 Look at the map and the cross section from **A** to **B** on the map. Add the following labels to the section:- Mount St Helen's, plates, plate movement.

4 Mark with arrows the directions of movement of the **plates**.

5 Look at the photos and try to explain how the eruption occurred.

6 Look at the LANDSAT image, a picture taken from a satellite. It shows vegetation in colours. It is taken after the eruption. Describe the effects of the eruption on vegetation.

CONTRAST AND CHANGE

u n i t

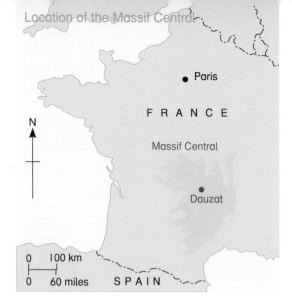

Location of the Massif Central

Paris

FRANCE

N

Massif Central

Dauzat

0 100 km

0 60 miles   SPAIN

People living in mountain areas have always faced special difficulties. Many young people have left these areas to live in the lowlands or in towns. Now governments are making plans to help these highland areas and bring people back to live there.

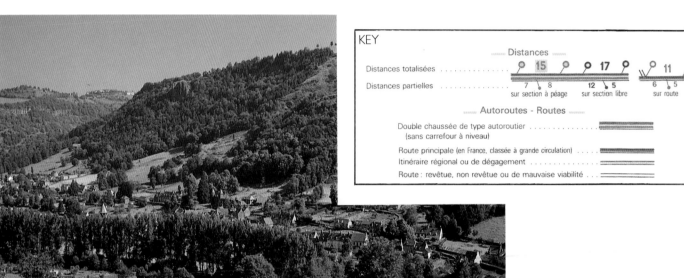

KEY

Distances

Distances totalisées . . . . 15 ⚪ ⚪ 17 ⚪ ⚪ 11

Distances partielles . . . . 7 ↘ 8   12 ↘ 5   6 ↘ 5

                                   sur section à péage   sur section libre   sur route

Autoroutes - Routes

Double chaussée de type autoroutier . . . .
(sans carrefour à niveau)

Route principale (en France, classée à grande circulation) . . . . .

Itinéraire régional ou de dégagement . . . .

Route : revêtue, non revêtue ou de mauvaise viabilité . . .

Village in the Massif Central

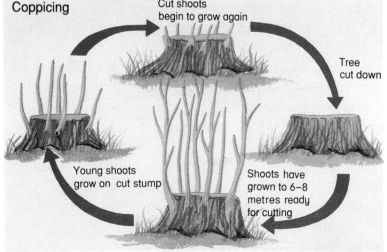

Coppicing

Cut shoots begin to grow again

Tree cut down

Young shoots grow on cut stump

Shoots have grown to 6–8 metres ready for cutting

The village

Dauzat is a small village in the Central Massif, a mountain region in the centre of France. For many years the people who lived there have been farmers. They kept cows, growing fodder in the valley to feed the animals in the winter.

The people also cut wood from the forested hillsides as fuel for their fires. They did this by coppicing. That is cutting a tree down and then when its shoots grew, cutting them. They could do this over and over again.

Clermont Ferrand 20 km ↖

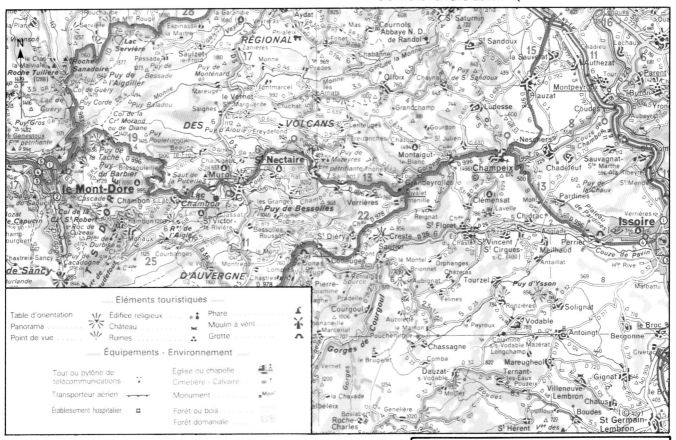

Michelin map of part of France, 20 kilometres south of Clermont Ferrand.
1 cm represents 2 kilometres.

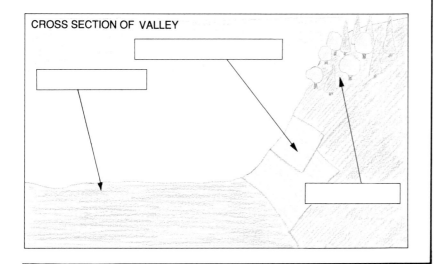

CROSS SECTION OF VALLEY

1 Look at the photograph. Write down a list of six words which you would use to describe your feelings about the village and its valley.

2 Look at the diagram of coppicing. It is drawn in the wrong order. Redraw the diagram putting the drawings and labels in the right order.

3 Look at the diagram showing a cross section of Dauzat.

(a) Redraw the diagram adding these labels in the correct place.

– WOODLAND USED FOR FUEL
– VALLEY FLOOR USED FOR GROWING FODDER FOR ANIMALS
– PASTURE ABOVE VILLAGE

(b) Draw in the village in the correct position.

4 Look at the map of part of France.

(a) Find Dauzat in the southern part of the map and describe its position.

(b) What does the symbol next to the village show?

(c) Join with a friend and write down six features of the area shown on the map.

The Region – The Massif Central

ALLIER AND LOIRE VALLEYS

In the bottom of the valleys there are rich soils where wheat and sugar beet are grown. In the lower slopes vineyards produce wines. Higher up, orchards grow peaches, pears and soft fruit.

LIMOUSIN

This area is a high plateau with wet cloudy weather. Nearer to Limoges the land is more fertile. Cattle are kept. Crops of hay, wheat and sugar beet are grown. Villages are scattered. Limoges is the main regional centre, famous for pottery and enamel ware.

GORGES DU TARN

The spectacular Gorges du Tarn lie in one of the poorest areas of the Massif Central. The Causses, as the region is known, is limestone. Water soaks through the cracks, dissolving the limestone and forming caves and gorges. The thin soil gives only poor grazing for sheep.

THE MASSIF CENTRAL is an upland region which lies in the centre of France. It contains a mixture of landscapes some of which are very spectacular. The Massif Central is traditionally an agricultural area. Although there are small areas of good land, much of the region is poor farmland. Farming is mainly pastoral – sheep and cattle farming on small family farms. There has been a steady drift of people from this upland area to the towns in

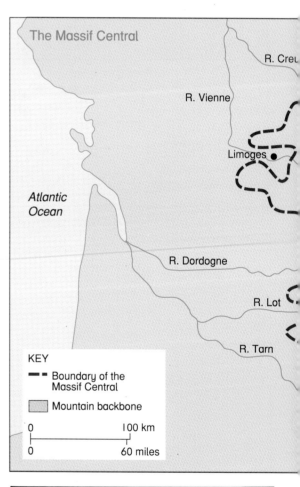

The Massif Central

R. Creu
R. Vienne
Limoges
Atlantic Ocean
R. Dordogne
R. Lot
R. Tarn

KEY
- - - Boundary of the Massif Central
⬜ Mountain backbone

0 _____ 100 km
0 _____ 60 miles

FLAT RUGGED ISOLATED
FORESTED RICH
MOUNTAINOUS VARIED
LOWLAND QUIET
OVERPOPULATED
VOLCANIC POOR BARREN
INDUSTRIAL

the surrounding lowland.

The government is trying to encourage people to stay. Increasing numbers of visitors are being attracted to the region. The tourists stay in converted cottages or small hotels. They enjoy the scenery and the craft industries. The work this creates will encourage people to stay. In turn services are improved, new farming methods introduced and forestry encouraged.

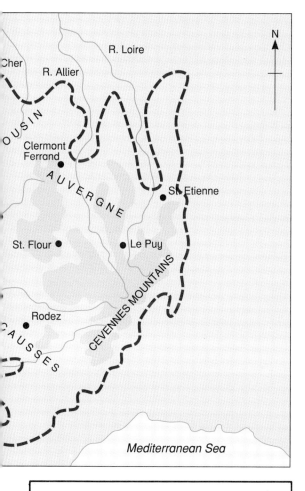

1 Look at the information on this page.
(a) List ten words from those opposite which you think best describe the Massif Central.
(b) Use the words in your list to write a short paragraph about the Massif Central.

CLERMONT FERRAND

This is the home of the Michelin Tyre Company, which employs 18 000 people. Clermont Ferrand attracts people from the poorer surrounding region. It is also an important industrial centre.

AUVERGNE

This is an area of thick forests and deep gorges. But the area is best known for its volcanic remains – there are over a hundred volcanoes here. Many lie within the 'Parc des Volcans', the largest national park in France. The volcanic rock makes a fertile lowland soil providing excellent pasture for sheep and cattle.

CEVENNES

Here is the most rugged country of the Massif Central. There are few villages in the mountain region because most of the people live in the lowland fringe. Sheep are kept, but towards the south the climate has warm summers and in the lowlands vines and market garden produce are grown.

Moving Out?

PROBLEMS OF THE PEOPLE IN DAUZAT

OLD WAYS OF FARMING

SCATTERED SMALL FIELDS

SMALL FARMS IN MOUNTAINS CAN COMPETE WITH EFFICIENT LOWLAND FARMS

FAMILY FARMS CANNOT AFFORD NEW MACHINERY

There have been many changes in the village. When I was young there was plenty of work for everyone with the cattle. This was a busy place.

" Life was always hard but the village wanted for little. We would go to market each week and buy what we wanted. "

" But now the big farms on the better lowland can produce leather and meat so much cheaper than we can. "

" The money we get from the government is not enough. "

" We feel cut off from the rest of France. The new motorways and high speed trains don't come here. "

" You can see the lack of money in the village. The houses are old and in need of repair and many of the barns and older houses are empty. "

We are all getting old. The young people are moving away. We grow some vegetables but there are a lot of new electrical machines to make life easier today. I wish we could afford them.

" It is sad to see the village in which we have lived all our lives dying before our eyes. "

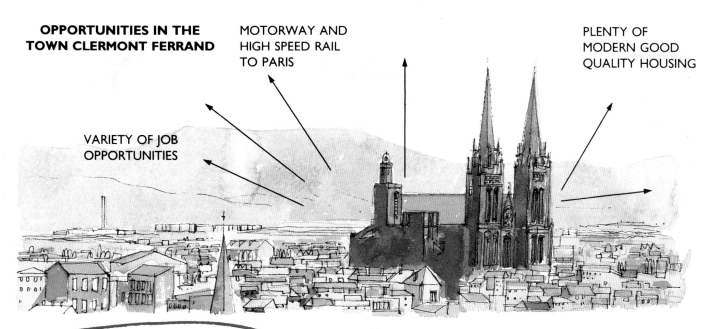

OPPORTUNITIES IN THE TOWN CLERMONT FERRAND

MOTORWAY AND HIGH SPEED RAIL TO PARIS

PLENTY OF MODERN GOOD QUALITY HOUSING

VARIETY OF JOB OPPORTUNITIES

"When we were married we left the village and went to live in Clermont Ferrand. There were new houses there which young people like us could buy."

"There were no jobs for women in the village. I did not want to spend my life working at home. I now have a job as a designer with a printing company."

"There were no jobs in the village. I had three brothers and we couldn't all take over the family farm. There were no other possibilities for work in the village. I work in the Michelin Tyre factory now and earn much more than I could in Dauzat."

"Things were pretty boring in the village. Because it was in a valley, TV reception was poor. There was no cinema or disco. We could only get to the nearest town occasionally as there was no transport unless we could find a lift."

"We hope to have a baby soon. There are better schools here in Clermont Ferrand and they are near where we live."

"I stayed in the village. I inherited the farm from my father. The others did not want it. I enjoy village life. I've always liked the open air, the scenery and I enjoy working with animals. We get to market once a week and have close family friends in the village. We all work together. It is the only life I know but it is hard."

1 Copy the sketch 'Problems of the People in Dauzat.'
Use the evidence from the villagers' discussion to add three more problems.
2 Copy the sketch 'Opportunities in the town of Clermont Ferrand'.
Use the evidence from the conversation with the young couple to complete the labels on the arrows.
3 (a) Decide whether you would stay in Dauzat or move to Clermont Ferrand. Give two reasons for your decision.
(b) Write down how you would feel about leaving your home and family to move to another place.

Planning for the future

The French government have made plans to help the Massif Central region. They hope that these plans will stop people leaving the region.

Transport

- a new motorway has been built between St Etienne and northwards to Paris.
- the railway from Clermont Ferrand to Paris has been electrified, shortening journey times.
- several roads including the N9 have been improved with many dual carriageway sections.
- local airports have been improved.

Improved services

New houses have been built in some settlements. Also to improve the quality of life, new transmitters have been built for better television reception, a better telephone service has been introduced, and winter snow clearing schemes in mountain areas have been organised.

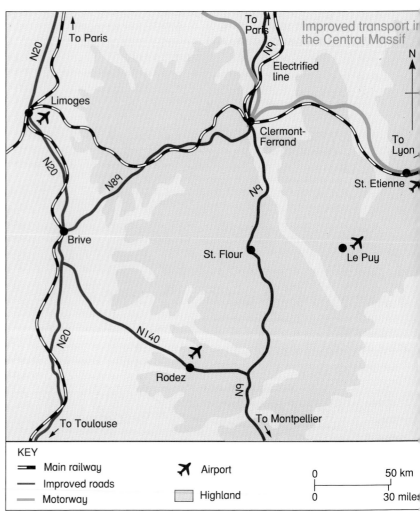

Improved transport in the Central Massif

KEY

Main railway	Airport		
Improved roads	Highland	0	50 km
Motorway		0	30 miles

Larger fields created by land reform west of Chaine des Puys

Farming

Young farmers have been encouraged to work together. As farms have been abandoned or left they have been grouped to make larger farms. In one area where flocks of sheep were 50 they are now three or four times larger.

Young farmers banding together have bought modern machinery bringing new areas in the valley into cultivation growing cereal crops.

Farmhouses and barns have been modernised using the extra money the farmers are earning and the grants from the government.

The poorest farming areas have been abandoned, as they would never be worth farming.

Trees have been planted on many of these areas for forestry.

VISIT THE NATIONAL PARK of the Cevennes and the **REGIONAL NATURE PARKS** in the Auvergne and Haut Languedoc.

THE VOLCANIC LANDSCAPE OF THE AUVERGNE

HOLIDAY COTTAGES

These parks have been designated to improve the natural beauty, flora and fauna of the region.

VISIT
THE
MASSIF
CENTRAL
THE HEART OF FRANCE

Auvergne

Cevennes

Gorges of the Tarn

Haut Languedoc

THE AMAZING GORGES OF THE TARN

There are hundreds of holiday cottages in the Massif Central. Old barns and farmhouses, renovated with the help of the government attract tourists to the country region.

THE VARIED LANDSCAPES OF THE CEVENNES

Roads throughout the Massif Central have been improved.

SPA TOWNS

The Gorges of the River Tarn are undoubtedly one of the most striking scenic features of France. The river winds below high limestone cliffs towering to over 500m.

There are many spa towns scattered through the Massif Central. Their mineral waters are known throughout France. Vichy is the most famous.

Tourism

The government has attempted to promote the Massif Central as a Tourist Area.

The old barns and houses which have been abandoned have become holiday cottages or second homes.

A National Park and Regional Nature Parks have been created.

New Job Opportunity

An increase in the planting and management of the forests has provided jobs for many young men who cannot be employed as farmers.

Craft industries and small workshops are encouraged. These could grow as the number of tourists visiting the area increases.

1 Look at the tourist poster above. Look at the pages on The Region – The Massif Central. Write down a caption for
(a) the volcanic landscape of the Auvergne
(b) the varied landscapes of the Cevenne.
2 Look through the information on this page. Use this information to make a large diagram, drawing, map or poster to illustrate 'PLANNING FOR THE FUTURE IN THE MASSIF CENTRAL'.

Glossary

Alkaline (Alkali)   A base which is soluble in water. It has a pH above 7. It turns litmus paper blue. (A base is the chemical opposite of an acid).

Amenity   A place which is provided as a service for people who live in an area, eg leisure centre, post office, community centre, car park.

Blue green algae   Tiny plants which grow and spread quickly in water. They use up oxygen needed by fish and other water life.

Business Parks   Areas set aside to be used for offices or small scale industries. The layout is planned to be as attractive as possible.

Bypass   A road which allows traffic to go past a town or city rather than through it.

Cash crops   Plants which are farmed and sold for money, eg tea or tobacco.

Climate   The average weather of an area over many years.

Colonies   Countries or areas governed by another country (colonies were often in tropical latitudes).

Colonisers   Countries which govern colonies (colonisers were often European countries).

Congestion   When there is so much traffic that it slows down or stops.

Decomposition   The rotting of waste and of dead plants and animals.

Derelict land   Land which is no longer being used and has been left to become overgrown and untidy.

Earth's plates   Slabs of the earth's crust joined together like pieces of a jigsaw puzzle. They can move slowly against each other causing earthquakes.

Environmentalist   A person who works to protect the surroundings in which we live.

Exports   Services and products made, mined or grown, which are sold to another country.

Farmyard slurry   Animal waste from farms which may be kept as a liquid in pits.

Fertiliser   Chemicals or manure which are spread on the land to make the soil rich.

Flood   When a river overflows on to surrounding land.

Ground water   Water in rocks under ground which can be reached by digging or drilling wells.

Habitat   Environment in which animals and plants live.

Hectare   Area of ground which is about the size of two hockey or football pitches.

Imports   Services and products made, mined or grown, which are bought by another country.

Lode   An ancient Fenland canal leading from the main river to villages at the Fen edge.

Market   The place where goods are bought and sold.

Mineral   A natural material which is mined or quarried from the ground, eg iron ore and copper which are melted down to make metal, and coal and oil which are burnt to provide energy and power.

Mud flow   Movement down a slope of lots of mud.

National Parks   Large areas of land used for conservation and leisure. Their boundaries are fixed by government.

Natural hazard   A great force of nature which is a threat to people on a large scale, eg earthquake, cyclone, volcanic eruption.

Overburden   Soil and rock which is removed before the mineral ore lying beneath can be mined.

Park and Ride   Traffic system used in many cities. Cars are parked in a large car park on the outskirts of a city and people travel by special buses into the centre.

Plantation   Large farmed area, often growing one crop, which is sold for cash, eg tea, rubber, bananas.

Pollution   Waste materials which make air, water and land dirty.

Radioactive wastes   Waste material from nuclear power stations which gives off harmful rays.

Reservoir   Lake made by people for storing water.

Residential area   A housing area where people live in a town or city.

Resources   Minerals, animals, plants, land and people which can be used to supply what we need, eg timber from trees, oil, water and skilled labour.

River channel   Area between two banks in which the river flows.

Route   The way taken to get from one place to another.

Seismograph   Machine used to measure and record the strength of an earthquake.

Sewage sludge   Muddy waste from sewage works.

Silage   Grass which is cut and stored for animal feed in the winter.

Source   The place where a river begins.

Subsistence crops   Farmed plants grown to be eaten by the farmer and family and not sold.

Tropical rain forest   Thick forest growing in hot, damp areas near the equator.

Water meter   Machine for measuring how much water is used.